# A LOVING DIVORCE

# A LOVING DIVORCE

*A Perspective of Compassion for All Relationships*

Moksha Books
P.O. Box 1834 , Staunton, Virginia 24402

A Loving Divorce
A Perspective of Compassion for All Relationships
By Lynda Miles

Moksha Books
P.O. Box 1834 , Staunton, Virginia 24402
Copyright © 2016 Lynda Miles

Cover by Gaelyn Miriam Larrick
Edited by Susan Arritt
Book Interior design by Bram Larrick
Back photo by Elaina Miles
Library of Congress Control Number: 2016900417
ISBN: 9780997163605

This book is dedicated to my children, who've taught me so much about love and life.

# CONTENTS

# PREFACE

I'm a bit of an iconoclast at heart. I often refuse to take things at face value. I refuse to conform for the sake of conforming. My heart seeks over and over again to lead the way. Most of the time, my heart seeks to say and prove that things *can* work in different ways and, many times, very well! My heart says, "Yes! Nothing has to be the way it is, so make it the way you want it!" Of course, I'm afraid sometimes. Of course, I wonder if I'm pushing myself too hard. I've come to understand about myself that to live and be happy, I must push, proving over and over again to myself that things can be different. Things can be better. I've learned that love is so much *bigger* than anything else. Absolutely anything is possible if I can open my heart, again and again, even when things seem insurmountable and I feel afraid.

Fred Rogers said, "Love isn't a state of perfect caring. It is an active noun like struggle. To love someone is to strive to accept that person exactly the way he or she is, right here and now."[1] That really resonates with

[1]    The quote by Fred Rogers is © The Fred Rogers Company. Used with permission.

me. There is nothing easy about what I'm sharing within these pages. It feels as though I have poured my blood, sweat, and tears into my internal personal work and my relationships. It has taken an amazing amount of help from others, effort, courage, research, vulnerability, raw emotion, processing, healing, acceptance, and openness. Sometimes I still feel anger, fear, sadness, and grief. Sometimes I feel selfishness and spite. I don't like feeling those feelings, but I allow them. I accept those feelings within myself and see them as signals. They are signals that there is something I need to express, process, grieve, accept, or change, etc. Sometimes, when all I feel is negativity and I'm stuck there, I do my best to find another way. Groping in what feels like a dark abyss, the alternative is always love. There's always a knob waiting to be turned. It's always within my reach—so simple and yet so difficult. It's like a shift within—a letting go and an opening up that takes place in order for me to find the alternative to the negativity I'm experiencing.

I think there is a belief in scarcity when it comes to love. Love is everywhere and there is *enough love* to support everyone getting along and working things out. There is enough love in the world to support and fuel loving and honoring. Love is infinite. It's not something you have to scrounge and reserve for the "perfect" relationships or "perfect" people (neither of which exists, thankfully).

Love has nothing to do with perfection. It has to do with acceptance and honesty. It has to do with listening and being heard, to the best of our abilities. There is no perfect listener or communicator. It is just about getting as close as possible to reality, to each person's realness, and learning to honor and embrace that as best we can. We will "mess up" over and over again—and love is about honoring that too. The word *mistake* is not one of my favorite words. I have to go through something to get to something else. I try to accept mistakes as stepping stones and leave it at that. When I began this journey, I thought it was our journey—my spouse's and my own. But it is not. Ours are two distinct journeys—mine and my spouse's. Love is the intertwining of those journeys. Love is the space in which things unfold. He is love and I am love. Love is the medium for growth and evolution. There is really nothing else but love.

From the darkest, most impossible senses of inadequacy can come the most amazing births of creativity and creation. It is often through our illusion of inadequacy that we feel compelled to create. And boy, do we create! We create from a field of love, knowing and wanting to prove, beyond a shadow of a doubt, that we *are* good enough, that we are enough, we are lovable, we are worthy. All the while, somewhere within ourselves we must *know* that we embody each of these traits—otherwise, why would we persist? Why would we half kill ourselves sometimes, wanting and trying to bring our gifts into the world? If we believed, really believed, we were not worthy, lovable, good enough, why would we bother? I think it's because we know somewhere within us, regardless of what others may seem to say, do, or feel about us, both past and present, that we are good enough, that there is perfection in our imperfection.

Imperfection itself is a perfect system, I think. It's a beautiful and infinite garden of discovery, growth, and opportunity. Think of the newborn, a perfectly whole being that has never been told it's not good enough. No one has yet convinced this divine creature that it's lacking in some way. It has needs, yes. But it doesn't feel wrong in its neediness, nor should it. I think somewhere, deep within, we know; we remember what we are, and we know we are not lacking in any way. So I think we seek to prove that to ourselves (and to others) through creating our lives and expressing life in the ways that we do. We are expressions of life, and we express life. We are what we came from and it is us. We are not separate.

# THE SKINNY

*The journey of a thousand miles
begins with one step.*
*~ Lao Tzu*

This book is meant to support love. It is meant to support you. Perhaps you're not married but have been in a committed relationship. Whatever you call your relationship, I mean to support your process. Maybe you want to improve your experiences within your current relationships and, if so, I think you'll find this book helpful. For simplicity's sake, I'll call my process "divorce," but it's so much more than that. Maybe if you're moving away from a partner, you call it "parting," or something else. Perhaps you're wondering if a kind of loving experience of parting ways is possible. I'd wondered too. Because what I wanted seemed so unusual—practically unheard of—and seemingly uncertain, I found myself feeling like an outsider to my own species. I felt alone. When I was considering a loving divorce, I could find no books on the subject. During my contemplation period, I found only one online article about the process. This was very helpful, but I felt I also needed living, breathing support. So, during a brunch with my dearest friends, I bravely bared my soul to them. In response, they told me that they knew of people who'd had loving divorces. One of them had had a loving divorce herself. They supported me. It felt so good to be supported by my friends, who, by the way, were all married. I must say, I think I have the most amazing friends in the world. They supported me in doing something that was seemingly opposite of what they were doing in their own lives, right then. I say "seemingly" because, really, what they were doing was what felt best to them, and in that way, my decision to divorce was no different than their decisions to be married. Their support and love was just what I needed.

I decided that a loving divorce was possible for me and I would settle for nothing less. I eventually stopped feeling like an alien being and started focusing on how to make this work! I can't tell you how to go about creating a loving divorce, as everyone and every relationship is different, but I can share with you what it looks like from my perspective and what my experience is. The things I share, aside from quotes, are just my perspectives—just the way I see and experience things.

The things I share are very personal, but I realize that I'm just one person; I'm not that important. Sharing deeply is important. Love, acceptance, understanding, and the possibility of helping others are important. In another light, I seek to "normalize" the experience of a loving divorce. I really think this type of experience can be the norm, not the exception. So here we go.

For starters, I had to process and let go of any possible judgments others might have about divorce. That was a tall order! My older siblings were all in lifelong marriages, and my younger siblings were also married, for at least several years. And what would my codependent mother say? I couldn't let others' possible negativity or fear about divorce taint my experience. This was going to be *my* reality, regardless of what other people felt or thought.

Much of the time it seems divorce is treated like a death and it seems common that people experience a lot of drama from the situation. I didn't want toxic feelings in my life and I'd do whatever was needed to make a loving divorce possible. I knew I'd hear "I'm sorry," repeatedly, when others learned that Brian and I were parting ways. I had to be able to know within myself that this comment had to do with the person's own experience, perceptions, and feelings about divorce. It had nothing to do with *my* experience, perceptions, and feelings about divorce. So before I shared this with the people in our lives, I wanted to be set in my own peaceful space—assert my boundary. Others' sadness and disappointment wouldn't affect my understanding and appreciation that we were making a decision that was best for both of us. When I did share, people were, by and large, very supportive. There were the usual expressions of sympathy and one comment I viewed as a possible judgment, but other than that, it was pretty non-eventful.

This separation/divorce was the next step in our lives. For me, it was a step toward realizing wholeness and greater independence, having healthier boundaries, and becoming healthier psychologically and emotionally. I wouldn't view this beautiful and meaningful process as a tragedy.

After the death of my father, I'd watched my mother move toward what seemed to be the next-closest man with whom she could be. She started talking about him within minutes of my father's passing. I thought it seemed shallow and desperate, even though I didn't want to have negative feelings toward her or what she did. Granted, she'd just lost her husband after a months-long, tiring, and trying illness—I don't think she was at her best! She had to do what she had to do. I didn't want to judge her; I just wanted to use what I saw as an "FYI," so to speak, a "note to self." I'd felt very disillusioned about what their relationship may have been, especially when I watched her take my father's money out of his wallet just a few moments after his last breath. I thought, "Wow, is that going to be me one day?" At that moment, I, like my mother, was afraid of being alone. I thought about divorce almost right away because I did not want that to be my level of emotional maturity and health when I was her age. I didn't want that to be my level of emotional maturity and health right then, either. Immediately and during the following months, along with grieving the death of my father, I asked myself and my husband some very difficult questions.

Did I want my whole life to be ruled by my fear of being without a partner? Did I want to stay in my marriage, when we had little to no common interests anymore? Did I want to stay within a marriage that, I felt, was characterized by enabling and senses of obligation and entitlement? Did I presently see the institution of marriage as something positive for myself? Did I want to be married at all? Did Brian want these things?

Parting ways was one of the best decisions I could make for myself and for my own personal freedom and sense of self-reliance in life. I didn't want my life to be dictated by my fears. My fears were just unwanted limitations that I could overcome and get through by facing them. As a result of this inner work, I'd be freer and open to more options in my own life. I'd be able to choose many things unavailable to me otherwise. Who knows what possibilities this sense of self-reliance and independence would allow in my life? I certainly didn't know, but I knew that I wanted my life to be whatever I felt I wanted, and I didn't want to be limited by my fears. As Carl Jung said, "If there is a fear of falling, the only safety consists in deliberately jumping." I knew if I faced the fear, worked through it with support from my spouse, dear friends, and possibly my counselor, I'd be able to do things I never thought I could. I had to free myself from myself.

# A LOVING DIVORCE

*The beginning of this love is the will to let those we love be perfectly themselves, the resolution not to twist them to fit our own image. If in loving them we do not love what they are, but only their potential likeness to ourselves, then we do not love them: we only love the reflection of ourselves we find in them.*[1] *~Thomas Merton*

Well, what is a loving divorce? A loving divorce, to me, is a parting that keeps love as the focus. So even if there are arguments, the preeminent goal is always to return to a place of love, understanding, and support with one another, as soon as possible. This is really just a continuation of what our focus was while we were married. Both Brian and I agreed to this focus and it made it easier than if only one of us wanted it. I think if I wanted a loving divorce and my spouse didn't, I'd do my best to remember that I have 100 percent choice over

---

[1] Thomas Merton, *No Man Is an Island*, (The Trustees of Merton Legacy Trust, 1983) 168.

what I contribute to the relationship. It may be difficult to maintain supportive and loving energy all the time, but I would do my very best. Not only is our divorce amicable, it is loving. We are a family; we support each other. A friend recently shared with me that she heard that one of the most important things for children is that their parents have a low-conflict co-parenting relationship.[2,3] I believe often people think what matters most is that parents stick together and stay in the same house—but it makes sense that the quality of the relationship is even more important than whether or not the parents cohabitate.

Throughout this process, and in life in general, it serves my best interest, and possibly the best interests of others, to understand that people who are hurting may do hurtful things (or things that may be interpreted as hurtful) and to try not to take it personally. Also, I try to remember that people are always trying to meet their needs in the best ways they know how. Some of these ways may be inconvenient or could be taken personally. Another's actions really have nothing to do with whether or not I'm "good enough." I don't need to take another's choices personally. I don't know what another person is seeking in life, what their "gaps" are—what psychological and emotional connections they are trying to make.

[2]  Christine Carter, *Raising Happiness: 10 Simple Steps for More Joyful Kids and Happier Parents* (New York: Ballantine, 2010).

[3]  Christine Carter, interview by Amy Tiemann, *The Mojo Mom Podcast*, podcast audio, April 16, 2010.

Many people are looking for approval, validation, attention, acceptance, a partner by whom they feel parented or needed, etc. It's my feeling that most often the person himself/herself doesn't know what it is they are seeking. So really, how is anyone else supposed to know? And is it anyone else's job to know? I don't think so.

Certainly, if we had no children it would've been easier to move on and not look back. Of course, even in the case of a childless divorce, a loving process would allow for much more growth and healing than the more common type of divorce would—at least in my opinion.

A bit about *love* . . . . I say that word and it means different things to different people. So I'll share with you, as briefly as I can, what love means to me, in the hopes that it creates a clearer concept of what I call "a loving divorce." I wrote a poem several years ago that captures it quite nicely for me, and here's a line from it: "Love is the space in which we partake . . . without expectation." This is what love means to me. It's the only way I can think about relating to another human being and feel really good about it.

So what would that look like in real life? Well, I decided that if I really loved someone, I would support him in having what he wanted for himself. I apply the same principle, if you will, to all my relationships, as best I can, including the ones I have with my children, family, and friends. I decided to be a supportive and honest person to those I love. I don't just bite my tongue or smile when I feel like crying, for the sake of being supportive. I believe that would be inauthentic. Besides, I must support myself equally, as well, as I'm just as deserving of my own love, acceptance, and respect as anyone else is. I'm as honest and authentic in my relationships as I can be, for the sake of having the healthiest relationships I can have. I share my feelings and/or concerns honestly, openly, and as respectfully as possible. I then look to the person and invite them to share more about why they want to do what they want to do, so I can understand them and support them better. Then, I give them my support, as best I can, in finding what they need to find on their unique journey. I may let them know that even though I'm having a hard time regarding their choice, I'll work through it and I'll be OK.

I feel we're all learning and growing all the time and we each need to be able to follow the direction we feel drawn to, in order to learn the most from this life and be most fulfilled. I allow myself to grieve and let go of any expectations that I may have had that are contrary to what my loved one wants for him or herself. This usually involves finding within myself something comparable to what I was attached to in the other person. It's a lot of work and can be very painful, but it's freeing and healing—and the rewards are most valuable. I'm not perfect in loving others, in any way whatsoever. This is just the focus I have for myself, as far as love is concerned, and it helps keep me pointed in the direction I want to progress.

Speaking of perfection, I've come to the conclusion, for myself, that we're all perfectly imperfect. What would be the point of life if perfection were ours? Everything would be a done deal, a snore-athon. We couldn't even watch paint peel as we'd have come up with a perfect paint. There'd be no discoveries. How awful and meaningless that sounds! If that's what perfection would look like, I'd choose imperfection any day. I'd choose discovery, uncertainty, and unpredictability a million times over the boring and meaningless mental picture I have of perfection.

This idea about being perfectly imperfect has helped me with self-acceptance, which has helped me to better accept others. We so often treat people the way we treat ourselves—and by cultivating more self-love, we can better love those around us. I find life to be so much happier this way. We don't know how long we'll live, so it seems to me that improving the quality of life is of the utmost importance. I want to be happy and my happiness is my responsibility. So yes, I love people in my own way and for my own selfish purposes: It makes me feel good! No one owes me a thing and I owe no one else—except that I feel I owe my children the best possible childhood I can provide them, as I chose to have them. I decide that I'm going to be happy today, and I do that the very best I can—by loving myself and others every possible moment of my life.

A friend shared with me an idea that has also helped me with self-love and loving others. It's the idea that there are shadow sides to all of the good qualities we have. For instance, I like to write and think about nonfictional issues. This is a very good thing, I think. But what are the negative aspects that feed this desire and ability? Looking at myself as best I can, I'd have to say that I have some negative feelings about our society and I want things to be different—better. I want there to be more compassion and more individuality. So, there's some cynicism on my part, as well as some inner struggle as I "hoe my own row" and do my best to follow my own heart. There's the potential for loneliness within me as well. Maybe I can be a bit withdrawn as I go deeply within to explore theories in psychology and the ways in which I and people in our society are unhealthy physically, emotionally, spiritually, and psychologically. So, the shadow aspects that support my interest and ability to write about the things I care about probably include, at times, my being cynical, lonely, withdrawn, and prone to inner struggle—perhaps sometimes also moodiness. This is just an example of the ways in which our gifts may be supported by things that aren't necessarily viewed as gifts—but that are, nonetheless, part of this human experience, and make possible our more useful qualities. I'm happy, regardless of these (sometimes) negative experiences, because it goes with the territory of doing the things I love to do. For the most part, I'm an optimistic and loving person—and like all human beings, at times I'm a real mess!

It seems like it can sometimes be a habit to view people as being either all good or all bad. I think that is one of the reasons it can hurt so much when someone disappoints us. We thought *this* person was different! A friend pointed out to me that we may learn this falsehood during childhood, as fairy tale characters are presented as being either all good or all bad. This might work in the world of fairytales, but it is not true in the world of humans.

To share with you a bit about what our loving divorce actually *looks* like, I think our family life is going well since Brian moved out. On the first Christmas Eve after moving out, he and his adult son slept over and we spent Christmas as usual. It was so nice! I loved that. It may not always be that way, and we may not want that at some point, but for the transition time, it was perfect. Then on Brian's birthday, we went to the movies and then all went out to dinner together. It was so lovely and one of the best birthday celebrations we've had for him that I can recall. It was so free and full of love. Sometimes Brian spends time here doing things with our two children, even if I'm here. We just each do our own thing and interact when we feel a need or desire to do so. It feels comfortable. It didn't feel comfortable at first, because we were adjusting our boundaries, but we've become accustomed to our evolved relationship. As I said, it may not always be this way, and that's OK. I'm grateful, in different ways, for the ways in which our relationship is evolving. We have so many patterns to heal and grow from that we can't possibly always do and want the same things. It just isn't realistic. We are growing and we are changing. I find it interesting that many of the areas in which we needed to grow were the very same areas in which we were compensating for each other. Not only that, I think we were blind to so many of those patterns because we'd been together so long. I couldn't see them until I didn't have him there to "save" me from needing to address them. It's been difficult, but it's something I really needed to do for my own growth and development as a whole and complete human being.

# GETTING TO IT

In the one article about a loving divorce that I found online, Rebecca Lammersen shared the 12 agreements that she and her husband made to help them be successful in their goal of having a loving divorce.[1] I think this is a great idea and my husband and I did something similar. When we were discussing separating, we had a book in which we would write our vision. We took turns writing in it. The decisions we made also went into this book. We didn't use the same agreements as Lammersen and her husband, but it was helpful to see their example of that process. Here are some of the agreements we made:

We'll get a separation agreement and we'll each pay half the fee.

We agree that this is a trial separation.

We agree not to get involved with other people during the separation, but if we do, we'll let the other person know right away.

We decide how to divide the possessions.

We'll make agreements on monetary support, health

[1]  Rebecca Lammersen, "How to Have a Loving Divorce," *elephant*, August 11, 2012, www.elephantjournal.com/2012/08/how-to-have-a-loving-divorce/.

insurance premiums, field trips, and tuition for our children.

We'll keep the life insurance policy current until the children are 20 years old. Then we'll change or end the policy when we both agree, or the one who still wants to keep it will pay the entire premium.

The living trust will remain in effect until one or both of us write a new one. If one person writes a new one, they'll let the other person know.

Other couples' agreements would look different, as they well should. We and our relationships are all unique.

A lot of pain came up for me at the time Brian and I were writing the agreements, as it did while we were just talking about and considering separation. He experienced some difficult feelings as well. It was nice to have time when we were still living together to develop and go over them. We also processed some difficult things we were feeling while we were in the stage of sleeping apart and still living together. It was important to allow space for our feelings, experiences, and concerns.

I'd had certain attachments to how I imagined the separation to be, and these ideas didn't match those of my husband. This was difficult for me but it had to work for both of us, so I needed to let go of those things, since he felt very strongly about his preferences. I'd shared why I felt the way I did, in every way I could. Then I needed to let go of it. What a difficult process that was! We'd been married for 15 years and together for 16 and a half, so I found it difficult to go from all to nothing—or what felt like nothing at the time. But it really wasn't *nothing*, and we had a nice and supportive relationship, even though a couple of relatively small details didn't match the vision I'd had then.

We had an attorney draw up the separation agreement, which would eventually become the divorce decree. We had to divide up the property. Material things aren't very important to me, aside from having a vehicle and a computer of some kind, so it was easy for me to tell Brian that he could take what he wanted to take. If an item was something that our children would miss, we'd talk with them about it. We wrote down everything that each person would keep and gave it to the attorney. Although this process was still emotional for me because it was making our choice a reality and it was a life change, it was nicer than fighting over a bunch of things. Seriously, if there was something he wanted, I gladly gave it to him.

We started looking for a house for Brian to rent or buy. I think even though it was somewhat painful, we were both looking forward to living apart. When he was looking, he took the children along to make sure they were happy with the house. Once he was moving in, we all went over together, which seemed so nice.

Pondering writing this book, during the summer of 2013, I wondered what to include in it. I'd spent almost the two previous years in personal crisis, dealing with the childhood I'd had. Beginning in 2011, about a year after the death of my father, I'd felt a new sense of safety and an opening in which I could face my trauma and wounds. He'd been the source of so many traumas and so many wounds that there was no way I could see to open up and heal while he was living and could still add to my pain. At age 32, I'd succeeded quite well in repressing the traumatic experiences for most of my life—to the point where I was unaware of their severity. I'd been in self-preservation and self-protection mode. I feel truly fortunate to have this sense of safety and support, which has been with me since shortly after my father died. I'd like to write about this experience at some point. I think it's commonly referred to as "midlife crisis," "the dark night of the soul," or even "fighting the dragon." But I call it "false identity dissolution." I'd had Stockholm syndrome my entire life, but I could only identify it once I'd healed from it. Stockholm syndrome, as I've come to understand and experience it, is a tendency for the victim to adopt the perspective of the aggressor, so they are less likely to be seen as a threat to the aggressor. Shifting away from my father's perspective completely, allowed so much more of reality to come to light for me. "A Loving divorce" and "false identity dissolution" aren't topics that are openly discussed, if they're discussed at all. I want you to know that, for me, this loving divorce wouldn't be possible if I'd not dealt with and healed from my own pain from childhood. In this book, I'll include many references to my personal healing and revelations that are relevant to my healthier emotional and psychological state now. It is this healing that has enabled me to live more compassionately than I'd been living before—and has helped this loving divorce become a reality.

This process of dealing with my pain helped the idea of our divorce come about in the first place. It might sound sad to you, but it is all about healing and becoming more whole, or rather, realizing how whole I *already* was. I see it as a positive process.

One of the main gifts I gleaned from my crisis was the realization that, as a child, I was and always had been "good enough." If my parents had ever communicated differently, through actions or words, it just was not true. If I'd ever inferred differently, from their actions or words, it just was not true. I was a beautiful and joyful child, and if my parents had ever behaved violently, abusively, or punitively around me when I was a child, that had to do with their own wounds. I was not lacking in a single thing. My blonde-haired, blue-eyed person, although small, always was enough. I'd been a symbol of love, life, and joy to my parents, as all children are. If they were too wounded and cluttered to see that, it was not a result of my falling short. I've always been enough.

Soon after these realizations, I understood that the ways Brian did not accept me were simply the ways in which he was unable to accept himself. That allowed me to begin my journey of self-love and acceptance, independent of his or others' approval.

I knew there were things I needed to work on within myself, things that were being pacified by the presence of a significant other. I had unhealthy boundaries because my parents had modeled unhealthy boundaries and had not afforded me my own boundaries as a child. I knew nothing else. I shared with my husband the things I wanted to change about our relationship. He didn't want to change them. What else was there for me to do? We wanted different things. Neither of us would have what we wanted within our relationship. I also knew I may not find what I wanted outside our marriage, but knowing that what we wanted was not possible within our marriage made it easier for us to decide to separate. We supported each other in having what we wanted. We wanted each other to be happy and fulfilled. I wanted to learn to give and receive freely because I associate giving and receiving freely with joy and fulfillment. There is no giving and receiving freely within a relationship where obligation and a sense of entitlement are present. In my opinion, that's just taking from each other, and each individual is doing it and allowing it to be done to them. Where is the joy in that? It isn't there, not for me anyway.

I'm reminded of the old adage "give and take." I think it's more like "take from others and allow others to take from you." I think it's possible to ask for what I need and for someone else to ask me for what they need. I think there is space for choice and space to do nice things just because I feel a genuine desire to do so. Doing something because I know it's expected of me is not a choice, really. The "choices" I see in that situation would be to (1) do the thing that is expected, whether I want to or not, or (2) make a real choice and if I happen to not want to do this task, then I can face the wrath of the other person's unfulfilled expectation. To me, neither of those scenarios seem like they have a foundation of freedom or love. I want a healthier relationship.

# TRANSITION

*Any transition serious enough to alter your definition of self will require not just small adjustments in your way of living and thinking but a full-on metamorphosis.[1] ~Martha Beck*

Understandably, in the beginning of my journey of being single I found myself feeling nervous about making enough money to support myself, managing a household, helping the children with their needs, and taking care of myself in the midst of it all. I felt like I was on overdrive for the first several months, alert and always on task. Eventually, I realized that I could survive and that I could take care of everything—and I relaxed. Brian was available to the children, almost whenever they needed him or wanted to see him, and that was wonderful. I was able to take care of my lawn and chores, work, and listen to and spend time with my children. I know it

---

[1] Martha Beck, "How to Deal with Major Life Changes," *O Magazine*, January 24, 2004.

sounds almost impossible, but it has worked well, I think. I'm so thankful that cooking and creating food is second nature to me, because when I'm having a hard time emotionally, the last thing I need is to let my diet go downhill. That will make me go downhill! It helps that our children are older and that they can do a lot for themselves. I help them and am available to be with them a significant part of each day, as I get my work done early in the day.

Since I was going through a life change, working for the first time in years was quite difficult. Fortunately, I have a job that's easy enough that if I cried every day, I'd still be able to get my work done. I was concerned about money, and Brian understood that. He was willing to reassess our agreed-upon child-support amount, should I find it insufficient.

I found that my mind was full of all kinds of sneaky, irrational beliefs, which undermined my well-being. I remember feeling that since no one was with me, I was unworthy of being with anyone. Intellectually, the idea of that feeling seemed illogical, but I still felt it. To work through this, I thought about some of my single friends and I thought about how beautiful and amazing they are! Was I so different from them? I came to the conclusion that I wasn't. Then I could see that I was not unworthy of being with someone, I just didn't happen to be with anyone. I changed my belief from one that caused me pain to one that I felt happy with.

Once I'd had time to be on my own, I had no one to defer to or to distract me. I had to look at my life the way it actually was, whether I really liked my life or not.

That was scary, but it felt like just what I needed to be doing. I took things one step at a time. I thought about how I wanted my life to be and I asked myself, "What do I need to do today to move in the direction of my goals?" It could be a tiny thing or a series of tiny things. I just needed to do something that would get me a step closer to where I wanted to be, each day. Sometimes it could just mean processing something or accepting something. Sometimes it meant asking someone for their help or expertise. That was hard to do, especially at first, but I became accustomed to it. Looking at my life without distractions was difficult, and at times I wanted to reach out for a man to distract myself with (and I did, sometimes) or to hopefully give some physical or emotional responsibility to. But that didn't feel good to me. It felt like a cheap out for me—inauthentic and, in a word, "bad." There's no magical savior or anything of that nature. My life is my life and there's no one who's going to rain in, sprinkle fairy dust around, and solve my problems. It felt scary to look at my life without being able to defer to someone else, or subjugate myself to someone else in some way—but it was just what I needed to do. It was the only way I could imagine becoming fulfilled and finding out what I was made of—just me.

I went through feeling afraid that I'd always be without a partner. Would I find anyone I'd really like to be with and who also wanted to be with me? I decided I needed to make peace with the fact that I might never find someone to be with! That sounds illogical, but it could be true—I just don't know.

I found a way to make peace with the possibility that I may always be without a partner. I decided that if I did whatever I could do to make sure I wasn't pushing people away or intimidating them, I'd be doing my part in being open to people—and I could be content with that. I'd be controlling the part over which I have power. I started asking myself each day, "Am I doing something to distance myself from people?" After a while, it became perfectly clear that I *was* behaving in ways that distanced myself from others and pushed them away. I found that I would use my intelligence to keep myself in a place of what felt like an advantage or a safe distance from other people. And I found out something pretty sad: I felt that my intelligence and knowledge were really all I had to offer others. Since my intelligence seemed to be my greatest asset, as a defense and a distancing behavior, when I felt the need, I think I was subconsciously "besting" people, whether using my intelligence or knowledge. I had to really look at that. It was sad and scary because I really care about so many of the lovely people toward whom I was behaving in this way. It was scary to acknowledge and then to change. I looked at the other gifts I have and the other ways in which I could enrich my life and the lives of others, independent of my intelligence and knowledge. I found that I have many other wonderful things to share with people. Seeing my other gifts helped me see more of others' gifts too! It was as if another whole world opened up and I could see so many things that I'd been blind to before. It feels new and scary to open up to changing something so ingrained and habitual within myself.

I worked on stopping that behavior and opening up to the idea that I had much more to offer than my intellect. It was extremely unsettling at first.

I also found that my not allowing others to help me was another way I was keeping myself distant from others. I'm a very independent person and it felt scary to allow someone to help me, if I didn't absolutely need it. I've found that sometimes it's nice to accept help, even if I can do something on my own. It is just a nice and connecting thing to do. I certainly help and offer help to others. Why did I only feel safe on the giving end of help? I think fear of vulnerability had a lot to do with that for me. I needed to push myself, a tiny bit at a time, toward opening up to others. I found that I loved being more open and flexible, once I was through the really scary part of gradually making that change.

Regarding meeting someone else, I had to ask myself if I was getting out and meeting people enough. I also had to ask myself if meeting someone was something I really wanted right now. I mean, with all I'm doing and working on in my life, what was I really able or willing to offer someone else? Maybe that was something that would be good for me to figure out before I met someone, because then I could be clear about where I was coming from.

I know all this might sound strange because my focus was on being alone and working through my fear of being alone. But these difficult and fearful feelings were coming up, regardless of my focus, and I needed to find a way to work through them. In my experience, opening up to my needs and feelings is the best way to help myself work through them. Had I stifled my feelings of negativity about being alone and my concern over not meeting someone I liked, I wouldn't have been able to progress through this stage very effectively or efficiently. I'd have been in a place of practically strangling the situation and not letting myself unfold organically. Allowing and accepting is important.

One thing that was sad and difficult for me, during this time, was realizing more fully how different my values seemed to be from the values of my family members. I felt sad about being seemingly so different from them. As I said before, all of my older siblings are in lifelong marriages and my younger ones have been married for at least several years or more. My mother probably could not even think of being alone without panicking. It was difficult to feel so different from my seven siblings and my mother! I'm one of the only ones who is not religious— there are possibly two others, younger, I think. I'm the only writer that I know of in my family, and the only vegan. I cried and cried about wanting to experience being on my own and about feeling so different. I cried about the fact that some of the biggest things that were so dear to my family members were just not important to me. I'm the way I am though, and I do love the ways in which I'm different. That's what makes me *me,* and not just an extension of my family (or of anyone, for that matter). I think, in order to fully become myself, I had to love myself more than I loved the idea of being loved for sharing my family's ideals. It boiled down to loving what I was doing more than I loved the idea of doing what I thought they might like me to do. It involved me knowing, for myself, that I know what's best for me better than anyone else does. This process has yielded a great strengthening of my inner authority and inner power. It's helped me become more confident and more decisive in my life.

# The Golden Rule

*The human heart, at whatever age, opens only*
*to the heart that opens in return.[1]*
*~ Maria Edgeworth*

Have you ever noticed that if you want something, often you have to be the one to give it first? I've experienced this so many times. This is something that so often people do not understand. Parents, for instance, will often try to make their children respect them, without actually ever respecting their children. They might yell at them, telling them to stop yelling! They might tell children to clean their rooms while their own room is disheveled. Can you think of times you've walked in on one of your children's activities or conversations and interrupted indiscriminately, demanding his or her instant attention? Have you then turned around and expected your child to say "excuse me" or to wait for your attention

---

[1] www.brainyquote.com/quotes/quotes/m/mariaedgew180863.html

when you're in the middle of something and they need your help? The bottom line seems to be "treat others how you want to be treated." It's the golden rule but so few people have the self-awareness to do it. It is not an easy task. My heart is warmed by the consideration and honor my children are able to show me. It is what they have been shown so it is what they know to do.

I think it is like learning a language. It is also about understanding that no one else is responsible for my feelings. My children are not responsible for making me feel better when I'm anxious about something, nor do they need to drop what they are doing so I can talk to them about, say, our full schedule or an upcoming trip. I need to ask and wait my turn and not communicate to them by my actions that what I'm thinking, feeling, doing, or saying is more important, in that moment, than what they are thinking, feeling, doing, or saying. It is no different with a life partner. Don't get me wrong, there are still so many ways I'm blind to the things I'm doing. Treating others as I want to be treated is just something I think is so important that I'm willing to keep this as a focus for myself, as best I can. Things work out best if I'm treating a partner, children, and friends the way I would like to be treated.

We are human beings and we have needs, and there is nothing wrong with that. It is one thing to make a request and quite another to make demands or use manipulation to get what we want. Asking to have a need met is very different than making demands and using coercion and/or manipulation to get those needs met. I think it is vital to make the distinction regarding the ways in which we go about meeting our needs. I feel that the ways we engage with others, when trying to meet our needs, is indicative of varying degrees of psychological, emotional, physical, and spiritual health—both for ourselves and our relationships. The ways in which we go about meeting our needs is worth noticing, and maybe even worth changing—especially if the ways we are treating others in order to meet those needs are ways in which we, ourselves, would not want to be treated. One self-check I've used to see if I'm using manipulation is, when making a request, to see if I would be OK with "no" as a response. If not, I'm using manipulation, communicated in my energy and demeanor. It is indicative of work that needs to be done within. We may even find that some of the needs we have are just really masking deeper needs, unresolved issues, or fears. Sometimes making sure a need is met is a way to enable ourselves not to work on our issues, or to not be vulnerable and express and acknowledge our fears. For instance, I used to have a need to have a clean and tidy home. I'm not saying this is a bad desire or an unworthy effort, but to make this a priority, at all costs— something is wrong. When I finally looked at the ways in which I was going about having that need met, I found that not only was I using coercion and manipulation to get that need met, I was stifling and limiting my children's creativity and freedom of expression. I was hurting them and our relationship. I was making the clean house the priority, instead of the relationships, and I wasn't caring for each family member's and my well-being equally. I was, in a word, narcissistic. I also found that what was at the root of this "need" was a deeply seated concern over what other people thought of me. So, basically, I was more worried about what the neighbors thought of me than I was about my relationships with my spouse and children. I'll sum it up in the most unattractive light: Regarding housekeeping, I was more worried about the opinions of the people who were practically strangers and cared very little for me than I was about the opinions of my own children and spouse—people who actually lived *with* me and loved me! We could go into many of the reasons why I was that way. There are quite a few. But I'll start from the point of awareness and the point of deciding to make a change. Changing my behavior involved strengthening my own inner authority about what was OK and what wasn't, and not handing over so much of it to people who were practically strangers. I'll talk about this in another chapter called "Boundaries."

# CHILDREN

Brian and I do our very best to consider our children in everything we do. For most of our children's lives, we've supported them and each other in having the experiences we've each wanted to have. Wherever we've wanted to visit, whatever we've wanted to learn, whatever we've wanted to do and have, we've tried to be open to anything and everything to see if we could make it happen. We've done our best to treat our children's desires and needs with equal importance to our own. So when Brian and I shared with them what we planned to do, we treated it as it was: an experience we wanted to have. We talked to them about what we wanted to do and why. We wanted to know what it was like to live on our own. We talked it over and listened and empathized with our children, rather than trying to "solve" their uncertain or negative feelings for them. We talked about what the new arrangement might look like and what ideas we had.

Children experience time differently than adults.[1]

---

[1] Susan Pease Gadoua, *Contemplating Divorce: A Step-by-Step Guide to Deciding Whether to Stay or Go* (Oakland, CA: New Harbinger Publications, 2008), 205.

For example, six months may seem like two years to a child. It is so important to allow them space to express their unique experiences and feelings. By this, I mean to be present with their feelings and not try to solve the problem right away, or assign meaning to them, for them. Listening and empathizing was helpful. I offered both my children the option to speak with a counselor if they wanted to. This option is always available to them.

We try to make it so our decision to live apart affects them as little as possible. They need space and patience to process what they need to process and they need to be able to go at their own pace. Since we really wanted to live apart, and we honored that, we honored them (as best we could) in the process. It seems best to honor them and their feelings and desires in as many ways as possible, at the same time we go about honoring ourselves by living apart.

No matter what we do and how hard we try, it is important for me to remember that I cannot conceive of my children's experiences or perspectives. I can listen, ask questions, ask for feedback, and so on, but I can't know what my children don't feel supported in expressing. They might not even know the things they don't feel they have room to express. Some of the feelings might be overwhelming to them and they may push them down, without realizing it. We likely have some familial patterns of which we are unaware, that may not be conducive to their complete honesty and their feeling completely supported. I certainly hope they feel they can express anything, and I do my best to be supportive and loving, in every possible way I can imagine.

We all travel together on family trips, as before, but we may not always do that. We have to see how it goes. We are always changing and growing and it may not always be something we want to do. If Brian goes on a trip and I'm not going, he usually invites our children to come along with him. They each decide if they want to go with him or stay home with me. If I'm going on a trip and Brian is not coming, the children each decide if they are coming with me or staying with him. It seems like a comfortable way to go about things and it has been good so far.

# ASSESS MYSELF

*Self-observation brings man to the realization of the necessity of self-change. And in observing himself a man notices that self-observation itself brings about certain changes in his inner processes. He begins to understand that self-observation is an instrument of self-change, a means of awakening.[1] ~George Gurdjieff*

Assessing oneself is immensely beneficial. Observing what was going on within me and then sharing that with Brian helped him to know where I was coming from and that my behavior didn't have anything to do with him. I asked him to share similarly. It is such an amazing difference when each person shares openly and honestly. We knew why the other was making some of the choices we were making, and we knew the things we were pondering or trying to work through. This was very

[1]   P.D. Ouspensky, *In Search of the Miraculous: Fragments of an Unknown Teaching* (Orlando, Harcourt, 1949).

important. Things would have been much harder to work through had this not taken place. If I wanted this sharing to take place, then I had to be a safe person for Brian to talk to. I couldn't judge him or condemn him. I needed to work through things and then be able to tell him that I loved him and that I wanted him to be happy—and I needed to be able to *feel* that. I needed to be able to feel that for my own sake, his sake, our children's sake, and the sake of our relationship. It was easy for me to feel that because I'd done so much work on my boundaries and having a healthy sense of self. If it were hard for me to feel that, then I'd need to work on myself until I did.

Noticing what feelings are present within, during communication, is so important. One thing I noticed that I needed to change in myself is that sometimes I would make snarky remarks to my husband. I knew they were snarky "mean" not snarky "funny" by the feeling I felt within when I was saying them. I felt a mean, yet yucky, feeling within myself when I spoke them. I realized that there were difficult, unspoken feelings and/or fears behind those snarky, passive-aggressive comments. I needed to dig in and be brave enough to uncover and communicate those feelings. It was more difficult and it took more time to do that, but I actually got somewhere when I did that, rather than hanging onto the negative feelings. The negative feelings were increased by the sense of frustration I felt by holding them down, instead of sharing them. Sharing these feelings was also helpful to Brian as he was able to understand me and there was probably even some helpful information there. Not sharing what I was feeling was not beneficial to either of us or to our children.

For the reverse of that, something I've found to be so helpful when I felt that Brian was being "mean" or saying something offensive to me, was to assess the energy I'd contributed to the interaction just prior to his offensive remark or behavior. I could always find that I had just said something unsupportive, sarcastic, or otherwise offensive. I would then own that and share that with him. I would apologize and let him know that when I'd experienced something negative from him, I discovered the way in which I'd helped elicit that very unpleasant comment, energy, or behavior from him. At first, it felt *so* scary to rewind the conversation in my mind and to look for my own negativity and how that contributed to my current unpleasant experience. Eek! I'm sure my ego wanted to point fingers and not take responsibility, if I were to find I was indeed at least somewhat responsible for what happened. I'm never really responsible for what someone else does or says. Brian did not have to respond to me with the same negative quality of energy I'd used to respond to him. But it is extremely important that I take responsibility for what *is* mine if I want to have more pleasant and constructive interactions. I was using passive aggression and I needed to own that. I wanted a more pleasant experience and I needed to deal with what was on my own plate so I could do my part. I needed to be an example to my family.

This is how I took charge of myself and took responsibility for contributing negatively to my own experiences.

If I don't want a negative experience, then I need to not communicate or behave negatively, unsupportively, or aggressively. That is what *I* own and that is where my power is. I have power over myself, not over someone else. I can *ask* something of someone else, but that is all. That is part of growing out of my egocentric self and developing healthy boundaries. It is part of growing up. It is painful and a lot of work. I find life to be so much better this way. I have more of a sense of inner peace that is independent of another's actions and choices. This to me is an aspect of true freedom.

I think it is important to know whether or not one's feelings about a current situation are being inflated by past, unprocessed experiences. It is important to be able to see if one's feelings, although important, are disproportionate to the current situation. This is an extremely helpful observation, because it is constructive and enables the person to work on what is really going on within him or herself. I use this often in my practice of self-assessment and observation.

If I need counseling, I usually have enough self-awareness to know that and then get it. I certainly would have benefited from counseling when we were separating. If I had known how I would have felt right after Brian had moved out, I would have planned on counseling and set aside the money for it. It is impossible to know how one will feel and it is important to keep in mind that divorce is a life change and it will not be completely stress-free. There will be things that will come up and need attention. Had I gone to counseling after Brian moved out, maybe I wouldn't have slept with men with whom I wasn't deeply relating. Sexually transmitted diseases and other issues can come into play if we are recklessly trying to hold down emotional baggage in this way. During this transition, there are likely other things that a person may resort to doing, although I read that having casual sex is a very common way to cope for newly separated people.

I've only been to counseling a couple of times in my life: once for post-partum depression and once for EMDR (eye movement desensitization and reprocessing) sessions when I was going through my crisis. It is interesting to think about how we are all psychological, emotional, and physical beings and yet we often completely ignore ever checking in with someone who specializes in psychological and emotional health, or, rather, in helping a person better navigate toward what is healthy for that particular individual. We may go to the doctor for our yearly physical checkups but completely ignore significant aspects of ourselves: our psyche and emotions! I compare the idea of waiting until in crisis to see a counselor to the idea of waiting to visit my medical doctor until I have a life-threatening disease or disorder, or some other crisis situation. It is so sad that in our culture, and in many others, seeing a counselor may be tantamount to taboo, failure, or getting a stamp on one's forehead that says "whack job." Counseling should be a natural part of life! It is responsible, healthy, and beneficial to talk to a good counselor, in my experience, and in the experiences of many others I know. What we are able to bring forth to the physical or visual world, including our behavior, is supported and fueled by the unseen—by our emotions and psyches. Of course we need to pay attention to those very important aspects of ourselves! I see so many people running around smoking, overweight, abusing their children, in miserable relationships, etc. (in my case, abusing casual sex, among other things), and I can't help but think that things don't have to be that way. I'm taking my own advice and I'm going to see a counselor—not because I'm in a crisis or abusing casual sex anymore, but because I want to. This is a huge step for me. I thought I couldn't afford it, but there is a counselor close by whom I hear is quite good; he charges based on income and has agreed to see me every other week. I think this will work for me! Although I do quite well by myself, I think I could really use a trained outside observer's take on things. You know what else? I really deserve help if I want or need it. It feels really good for me to allow that understanding and compassion for myself.

Frustration with some personality traits and behaviors of a sexual partner of mine led me to do some reflecting. Interestingly, I realized that the things I saw within this person—the things that I was struggling with—were things I discovered to be also true of myself. I've written about and felt, for several years, that we are all mirrors for one another. What we see in others that we don't (or do) like are often the very same things we share in common with them. One of these things I discovered about myself was that in some ways I was emotionally unavailable. It sounds so icky, doesn't it? Well, it doesn't *feel* great either.

I read that one of the root causes of emotional unavailability is having felt unsafe emotionally as a child. Another cause, also stemming from childhood, is a person's belief that they aren't worthy of being loved for all that they are. A woman struggling with this, for example, may feel that only certain aspects of herself are lovable— and that if someone really knew everything about her, they wouldn't love her. This can lead to not being open and receptive to others' needs, possibly because of preoccupation with this constant worry. It may also lead to compartmentalization (managing information), in an effort to try to make sure others see her in only a certain way. Maybe there would be other rather deceptive behaviors a person would resort to, as well. Sometimes a person may withhold sex because just being involved with someone emotionally or living with a life partner is overwhelming enough. Some emotional unavailability can also be evident in people immersed in caring for plants or animals.[2] Emotional unavailability can be quite a difficult experience for all the people involved, I think.

There are many "flavors" of emotional unavailability, meaning that it can manifest in different ways for different people. For me, when it came to romantic partners I would reserve my inner resources for myself. Since I wasn't going to ask for help with my needs from my romantic partner, I reserved what emotional nurturing I had within me to use to take care of myself. This

---

[2]   Kortsch, Gabriella. *Emotional Unavailability & Neediness: Two Sides of the Same Coin.* Createspace, 2014.

dynamic makes everything more one-sided and is really not a win-win, or a very healthy way of relating. It is also not connecting. I'd just felt unaccepting of my needs and I didn't feel as though I could ask anyone to help me meet them. It was so scary to start opening up and asking for and offering help and support. I had to take baby steps and deep breaths. I also needed to become emotionally available to *myself*. I needed to be able to offer myself true and completely accepting empathy when I was feeling sad or upset. You know that observer within? I've heard it referred to as the "witness" among some religious people. (It could also be what is referred to as the "higher self.") Well, I found that this observer within can actually be empathetic and compassionate to me. It can actually give me permission (acceptance) to cry, even though I might not know why I feel sadness. I know it sounds strange. Once I became more emotionally available to myself, my way of being began to change and I could experience my feelings more in the moment, instead of separating emotionally and only engaging with people intellectually. I had my own support system within, and I wasn't relying on outside validation as much, from moment to moment. Don't get me wrong, I still want and need that from others. It's just that now, I don't have to be as dependent on that because I've found it within myself. Life became safer, richer, and more real in the present moment. It made such an amazing difference in my quality of life and how I processed pain. I just allowed myself to feel, rather than trying to think my way out of feeling. I've found that so far, feeling pain is a pretty quick way through pain. Grappling with it intellectually could actually lengthen the process, as one of my friends often says. It has also allowed me to be more compassionate toward others. I'm more genuinely concerned for others, for the sake of just wanting to help another person feel better or feel cared about. I think that with being more open to asking for help, and with this inner observer being a source of compassion, I'm less afraid of "running out" of inner resources. I'm genuinely interested in what people have to say and what they are thinking. That is a very good and connecting feeling. I really like it! I think it might be safe to say that I really love it.

This may be obvious to you, but I want to mention it because of its high importance. A healthy diet, full of whole, unprocessed, nutrient-dense foods will go a long way to help a person feel good and have a better handle on reality and his or her emotional impulses. They will also help a person to mature gracefully and with fewer health issues, which improves the quality of life. A healthy diet, exercise, and sufficient sleep will help a person to be able to cope better, be more evenly tempered and less reactive.

Having a life rich in loving and supportive friends makes, and has made, *all* the difference in my life! I love and need my friends. I couldn't imagine life without them. I've noticed that my collection of friends seems to be comprised equally of both males and females. For me, I think this is very healthy because I'm unafraid of having friendships, and even close friendships, with men. It seems I'm allowing myself to navigate freely to where I feel drawn regarding friendships, and that, to me, is a sign of being more and more comfortable with men and with my own so-called "masculine" qualities. I say "masculine" because what I'm talking about are qualities in myself that are human qualities, but that culture and probably my family have deemed "masculine." I think I'd repressed many of them for the sake of fitting in and being "accepted," as a female, in my family and in our society. Some of the qualities I repressed might be my ability to show or feel anger without feeling guilt over it, decisiveness, assertiveness, my ability to be vocal about my feelings and desires, asking for what I need, and my ability to take on physically challenging activities.

My father had also shown me, when I was very young, that masculinity was dangerous and could hurt people. I healed from this, partly by understanding that he was not a monster but that he was an unhealthy human being, and it has made a huge difference. I'm embracing more and more of my own qualities all the time, and this is reflected in the variety of wonderful people I call friends.

To summarize, I think that good-quality food, exercise, sleep, supportive friends, and self-assessment are all so important, for many reasons, and they would certainly help toward having a successful loving divorce or relationship.

Lastly, I want to mention the idea of reflecting on personal choices. I shared this practice with a friend years ago, and she said it made such a difference in her life. It has made a tremendous difference in my life. It addresses resentment that we can sometimes feel as parents or spouses regarding all the responsibilities we seem to wake up one day and realize we have. It addresses the day-to-day tasks that can sometimes leave us feeling overworked and under-appreciated. For me, it started with nursing my babies. Nursing on demand, for a new mother—or any mother, for that matter—can be quite literally a draining task! I remember feeling tired and so worn out. Then I realized how important it was to me to be doing that for my children. Once I internalized the choice and meaning connected with nursing my babies, it took on a feeling of choice, instead of a feeling of task. Such a simple shift in perception made such a difference to me and the way I felt.

Another thing I applied this sense of choice to was doing the dishes. This was something I loathed for many years. Even though I've always owned a dishwasher, dirty dishes were a source of dread and resentment for me for years. I hated doing the dishes. I finally started to address this thorn in my side. It took months of trying different things. In one attempt, each person in our family had his or her own set of dishes that they were responsible for. Everyone—including me—ended up hating that. I tried a schedule of each of us emptying the dishwasher and refilling it, while watching my children struggle to accept that task being foisted upon them. I think I tried a couple more things before I finally landed upon a different approach. I didn't like how I felt, lording over everyone else in the family, making them follow a dish schedule or dish rules. I finally assessed how much it meant to me to have the luxury and convenience of being able to grab a clean dish, and then later set it in the sink. I thought about how much it seemed to mean to everyone else, too. I realized that for this freedom of everyone just grabbing and using dishes, without the unpleasantness of lording over others, I would be willing to donate thirty minutes of my time each day. It was worth that much time to me.

So one day when the sinks were full of dirty dishes and the dishwasher was full of clean dishes, I timed the process for myself. Guess what? It took me twenty minutes! Imagine all that fussing, griping, and trial and error for something that took me less than the amount of time I was willing to donate for that convenience! I learned a lot from that experience and from the experience of actively choosing to nurse my babies. I've subsequently applied this process of choice-making to almost everything— except now it is usually a much faster process than the dirty-dish debacle was. Applying this process has been a great reliever of resentment, and it has helped me to decide to adopt, modify, or abandon different tasks, depending on how I feel about the value of each one.

# THE CEREMONY

*He who binds to himself a joy*
*Does the winged life destroy;*
*But he who kisses the joy as it flies*
*Lives in eternity's sunrise.*[1]
*~William Blake*

About three and a half months after he moved out, Brian was considering allowing a woman and her young son to move in with him. We both know her, at least a little bit, and she is a beautiful and loving person. We both really like her and she needed a place to stay. All kinds of feelings came up for my son and me, but because Brian was honest and told us what was happening and what he was considering, we were all able to talk about it and work through it together. We shared our feelings and concerns. It really helped.

This impending event brought me to a place where I felt compelled to look inward and see if I really wanted to be with Brian or not. Had I discovered that I did

[1]  www.poemhunter.com/poem/eternity/

want to be with him, it didn't mean he'd want to be with me also. I just needed to know what I wanted so I could speak my truth, whatever that may be. That was a difficult process, especially with the idea of the woman moving in with him on the horizon. A counseling session probably would have been ideal, but due to the circumstances of being on my own for the first time in my life, I decided to take some time to myself and go into my bedroom to think and ask myself questions. I did this a couple times, a few days in a row before I knew what my answer was for myself. My answer was no, I did not want to be with him anymore.

Even though Brian and this woman were just friends at that point, I could imagine their relationship developing into something more. I find it particularly interesting that even though I'd been with someone else, the thought of Brian being with someone else was somewhat difficult for me. I just decided this was so hypocritical that there was no way I was going to stand for having that possessive feeling within me—plus, it was miserable! I had to think of a way to get through these feelings and it seemed that redefining our relationship, somehow, would be a good way to help me get started. I needed a space in time where we could state "that was then, this is now."

I asked Brian if he were willing to have a private ceremony with me, one in which I could declare my new commitments to him. I explained that I needed a sense of a "that was then, this is now"—a ceremony to mark our transition. People have wedding ceremonies: why not also have loving separation ceremonies, redefining the new relationship? I explained what I'd come up with for the ceremony about a week ahead of the date we'd set. I shared this with him so he'd know what to expect and so he'd have time to prepare if he wanted to share something or add anything to the ceremony.

When the morning of the ceremony arrived, I went to his house. We "smudged" each other before we began the ceremony. Smudging, as I understand it, is a pre-ceremonial cleansing tradition from Native American and other cultures in which bundles of dried sage are lit and then smolder, spreading a rich and fragrant smoke. A smoking bunch of sage is then waved all around a person's body. It is said that this cleanses negative energy from the auras of the participants. Whether or not this is true, I don't know. I think at the very least, the scent and sight of the smoke helps bring participants' attention to the present moment, which of course maximizes the impact of the experience of the ceremony.

After smudging, Brian and I then placed our hands palm to palm with one another, while sitting and facing each other. We kept our hands open to signify that we are with each other but not holding onto each other—that we love and honor one another by choice. To me, it was also a symbol of my trusting of life and the nature of the universe, a symbol of acceptance.

While our hands were over and under each other's, I told Brian that I would always try to be as understanding as possible, no matter what happened. My main fear was that he'd find someone else and forget about our children—and forget me, too. I let him know this fear and that I'd decided for myself that I would be OK if that happened and that I would do my best to help our children be OK. I let him know that I would understand that he would be having a hard time if he were to do something like that, and that I'd try my best to be understanding of him. He assured me that would not happen and we continued.

We shared a few more things—among them were elements of our relationship for which we felt gratitude. These were ways in which we felt the other had contributed to our life, things we greatly valued and learned from each other. It was a warm time, with many tears—mine anyway. After we shared all that we wanted to, we each lit our own candles to symbolize the beginning of this new relationship, one in which freedom and honor—*love!*— were the main focus. This is unconditional love I'm speaking of, an immensely powerful kind of love. This is a love that transforms through acceptance and gratitude. It is a love that feels really, really good, in my experience.

# My Vow of Celibacy

This chapter is really an extension of the chapter about assessing myself but I believe the vow should have its own chapter. Something that would have been helpful for me to assess, when Brian first moved out, was how I found myself feeling as though I were ready to climb the walls. I felt as though I really needed sex! I'd had great sex with him for almost as long as I'd known him. I found myself having difficulty going without sex.

So I had approached him with the subject, a couple of weeks after he moved out, and we had a substantial conversation. I let him know that I wanted to have sex and that I would be very happy to do that with him, if he wanted to. I mean, we'd always had awesome sex and there were no risks with him since we'd been exclusively with each other for so many years. If it was sex that I wanted, I would of course check in with him first. He let me know that he felt he was "going in another direction." I said, "OK." Then he said, "But I don't mind if you want to be with other people."

I thought this was very kind of him and I appreciated knowing his feelings, even though I hadn't asked for his

opinion. I asked for what I felt I needed from him, and if
he wasn't willing to help me in that area, I wasn't willing
to go without. In that moment, I'd felt completely over
the aspect of marriage in which I felt that meeting my
sexual needs was dependent upon Brian. It felt as if he
had decided for me, for all those years, whether or not I
would have sex, because it depended on whether or not
he wanted to have sex. I had a very high sexual energy
and his level of sexual energy is lower than mine. I cannot tell you how many times I wanted to have sex and he
didn't.

During this conversation, I also wanted to check in
with him about his "box" situation: Would he draw lines
in the sand and make a mental construct surrounding
my choice, and assign a definite meaning to it? In order
to find out, I asked him, if I slept with someone else, did
he feel that he would never want to be with me again?
I wanted to know what the gravity of my decision was,
concerning him. He said that no, he didn't feel that way—
my being with someone else would not negate his openness toward me and the possibilities.

This felt good to me; I was glad Brian was able to be
that open-minded and supportive. It was at that point in
the conversation that I let him know that I planned to
have sex, even if it were not with him. I don't know how
long he thought it would take, but within a week of that
conversation, I'd slept with someone else—a friend I'd
known for about six months. Even though I didn't hide
anything from Brian, he didn't know that I'd done that
until a couple months later, when he asked me. I told him

yes, that I had been with someone else. He said, "Oh, well it didn't take you long." I said, "No." I think it was, at that point, when the separation shifted to a new level for him. He seemed to be less affectionate after that and I accepted that this was the way he needed to deal with things. This is how I perceived things anyway. After a couple months, he initiated hugs again, so I think he just needed some time to adjust to the way things were.

Had I felt centered enough to assess myself more insightfully when Brian first moved out, I would have realized that I was using sex to replace my own acceptance of my body. I'd had children and I'd never made peace with my post-pregnancy body. I'd also been using sex to hold down a multitude of issues that I needed to deal with. So, for my sake and for the sake of having healthier relationships with myself, men, and sex, I decided to make a three-month vow of celibacy.

To allow the unprocessed and unpleasant emotions to surface, those that were being pacified by my having sex, I needed to stop having sex! OK, there were likely other ways to make progress here, like perhaps therapy, but this was a sure-fire and efficient (and free!) way to allow these things to come to the surface. For some people, sometimes it's not sex that is holding down their unpleasant, unprocessed emotions. Some examples of things that could be holding down unprocessed emotional experiences could be smoking, coffee consumption, narcissistic behaviors, overeating, and alcohol consumption—or a combination of several things. The list goes on. We all have our drug(s) of choice, so to speak. My main one, for most of my life, happened to be sex. Part of why this was, I discovered, is that I was not comfortable with my own needs or expressing my own needs. Sex was a way for me to have many of my needs met, without actually acknowledging or addressing them directly. Sex is something that is by and large, I think, more acceptable than expressing needs. Men often like it when women want to have sex with them. I found having sex much easier than saying something like "I feel a need for companionship, connection, affection, or deep conversation. Does that work for you?" Sex seems to be often something that men go for, without needing too much persuasion and without dishing out criticism. It's a lot less vulnerable a need to express. Just saying, "I really like sex," seems to be a lot less threatening than expressing a need that is seemingly not as primal and straightforward. I also think sex more often seems to have men's "stamp of approval." Expressing "neediness" doesn't seem to be as acceptable.

At the beginning of my vow, I did a lot of grieving. I was amazed at how old some of the beliefs I had were. I must've held some of them since I was a child. I grieved the relationship I *wished* I'd had with my father, one in which safety was central. It was a fantasy I'd had for I cannot tell how long! I didn't even know how long I'd had it. I know it sounds strange. I'd already grieved the relationship I'd actually had with him, both the good and bad aspects of it. I think I'd been looking for this fantasy relationship with men. (Good to know!) It was a painful evening of tears and tightly contracting stomach muscles. I was amazed that I would kind of howl and wail like a small child over some of the things I processed. In fact, only after my father died did I ever make a sound when I cried. I guess I didn't feel safe making a sound before, calling attention to myself. There were all kinds of "leftovers" to let run through me and to feel. I grieved the fact that I could not be a child anymore and that no one would take care of me. I had to face that and let that cycle through me. There was the matter of the fears of abandonment and engulfment. Those were particularly difficult. A friend of mine was most helpful during this time.

I had really missed one of my sexual partners during this vow, and had a lot of difficulty telling him that and asking if we could spend some (platonic) time together. That was horrific for me to communicate. I remember howling and crying so hard over this. I remember my stomach muscles tightening and even cramping as I was processing this. This must've been some deeply embedded, long-held pain that I was dealing with. I was glad I was able to ask and receive a nice and supportive response from this friend. It was so scary. I really must not have been able to express needs to my father growing up—or at least I believed wholeheartedly that I could not. Asking for something or sharing my feelings has been so difficult for me to do with men. Asking to have my needs met (or somewhat met) through sex was so much easier for me to do! There was a lot of father transference for me toward this friend of mine. I was aware of that when I'd met him almost a year before, and I'd worked through much of it immediately because I could identify it; but I obviously hadn't worked through all of it. It is interesting how knowing that conceptually didn't mean that I could think my way through it. I still had to process things before I could move through it, heal, and move on. Fortunately, this person is a dear person and he's been so supportive and kind. I've worked through so much during the short time we've known each other. I've shared with him that there was transference at work, so at least I've been honest. Transference, as I understand it, is basically when we take the unprocessed and unintegrated experiences from our lives, especially from childhood, and we, usually at least somewhat subconsciously, direct that unresolved experience to a new object (person) so that we may work through it. People do this all the time. It is a part of life and it can be an extremely powerful and often difficult experience.

It is said that dealing with our unprocessed experiences is the work of the stage of human development known as *midlife*, and transference happens to be a very common way that the pain and unprocessed baggage comes to light. There are varying degrees of transference that are part of virtually every experience we have with others. I think transference is part of what helps people to feel compassion for others, because we often think of how we would feel in a similar situation. In such a case, the focus is reversed: We somewhat transfer the experience of another to our self, and through that, we are able to offer empathy and feel compassion.

Another thing I realized is that we are often looking for a parent within our partners. We want someone to make us feel safe. It was interesting for me to realize that safety is an illusion and I was longing for that safe feeling that my mother or father may have provided me, when I had a boo-boo or something. Sure, I may have really felt that at some point growing up, but if it weren't for the fact that I'd had little life experience, I would have known that there wasn't any way on earth to be truly safe, no matter who was watching out for me. I'm not saying feeling safe isn't a lovely thing. It is—and for children who get to feel that, I think it is beautiful. It is natural for young children not to have an inner authority and to look to the parent to see if something is safe and to rely on their judgment for their sense of practically everything. I wonder how much I actually felt that sense of safety and miss it, or just long for it because it is a natural human desire to want to feel safe. It was important for me to realize and internalize that there is really no safety. As a parent, I knew that I could watch my toddler very carefully, but that a tumble or boo-boo was never preventable. Understanding that the protector or parent is so often also a source of injury to their children—emotionally, psychologically, and sometimes even physically—is very helpful in terms of becoming disillusioned to this fantasy and longing of safety.

It was quite a revelation to realize that I had a minor sex addiction. I think many people do, but they've just been having orgasms much of their lives and don't realize what those sex hormones and chemicals being released into the body are allaying each time. There can be a lot going on under the surface. I don't think there can be any "rules" about how much sex is too much sex, or what is good for people and what isn't. I just knew that I could be quite obsessed with sex and I didn't want that addiction to rule my life. It was taking up a lot of head space and disordering my priorities—basically ruling my life.

My pattern of needing sex to allay negative feelings of which I was unaware, and to meet my needs, is so common. It is said that men, in general, resort to sex as a safe way they can express their tenderer, more sensitive sides (and meet some of those needs). Men are not usually supported to share feelings, to cry, or to show their "weak" emotions in any way. Anger seems to be the emotion that is chosen more often. Of course, sadness, hurt, fear, nurturing, and tenderness do not belong to females. These are human qualities and emotions and they belong to everyone (they belong to other species as well). Gender should not dictate which aspects a person is allowed to embrace within themselves, and share with others. It is so sad when people aren't supported in expressing their full humanness. Gender stereotyping runs so deep within our culture and personal histories that it can be difficult to see the ways in which we are perpetuating it each and every day.

I'm certainly happy to be in a place within myself where I feel I can have much healthier relationships with myself and men, and a much healthier relationship to sex. Just think, subtle and subconscious negative feelings, beliefs, and baggage won't be a significant portion of what is initiating my desire for sex! I can desire it for the sake of the experience. How wonderfully positive, from inspiration to finish!

# BOXES

*Events do not have meanings. Events are events,*
*and meanings are thoughts. Nothing has any*
*meaning save the meaning you give it. And the*
*meaning you give to things does not derive from*
*any event, circumstance, condition, or situation*
*exterior to yourself. The Giving of Meaning is*
*entirely an internal process- entirely.[1]*
*~ Neale Donald Walsch*


I have experienced for myself and also observed other people putting relationships into "boxes," or mental constructs. I think of this as categorizing so as to assess things and to be able to prevent ourselves from experiencing pain. Maybe what I'm thinking of as boxes are really types of judgments. It might be common in high school for someone to wear a ring on a necklace and to say to themselves and to others, "I'm in a committed

[1]  Neale Donald Walsch, *When Everything Changes, Change Everything: In a Time of Turmoil, a Pathway to Peace* (EmNin Books, 2009).

relationship so all attracted people, keep away from me and my partner"—or simply, "I have a boyfriend!" There may be some arbitrary rules that are insisted upon by one or both partners. For instance, the relationship may mean to one partner that they must always reserve Saturday nights for each other. The demands (if they are not requests) we can make of our partners to perpetuate our own individual illusion of safety can include all kinds of things. I think it is because people want to create a feeling of security for themselves. It can be a lifelong human desire, I think. To me, it is basically saying, "If you are serious about being in a relationship with me, then it must look like this, and you must do *a*, *b*, and *c* in order for me to feel safe enough to love you." We often continue that into adulthood using a wedding band. We usually have a list of rules that go along with this symbol as well. Along with the things included in wedding vows that people try to adhere to, there can also be more-subtle or not-so-subtle demands made. One might insist that the other always call at a certain time or make certain that the other always consults them about purchases. I think it is to create a sense of safety and security.

The sense of security and safety that we all want to feel can sometimes lend itself to a person putting relationships, experiences, people, and behaviors into boxes. I hear people saying things like "if he doesn't love me now, he must've never loved me" or "he must not be 'the one.'" There is the idea, for some people, that there is a (possibly) attainable, forever-safe place that involves consistency and a loving partner. Ideas of "meant to be" and "soul mate" are common. Often something that goes along with this is that if a person sees that anything doesn't fit their picture of safety, love, and security, it's then time to discount everything in one giant, hurtful heap. For instance, if someone believes that there is one picture-perfect relationship and something is not right with what they see in their reality, they may discard all of the good things and rob themselves of being in the moment and enjoying the love they have or have had. I remember reading about someone who thought her partner never really loved her because he doesn't love her now. Interestingly, we might argue that unconditional love doesn't stop, so this may be true. Leaving that aside though, could we sit with the idea that we are all human beings, meant to evolve, learn, and grow every single day? What is true for us one day isn't true for us the next, necessarily, and that is OK. It doesn't make it any less true for our past selves. It was real and true at some point. That is part of growth and discovery. So if a person loved you once and no longer does, then throwing it all out because it doesn't fit into a box—a perfect picture of forever—seems so sad. What if the love *was* true—it was real at some point? Can we just put that into a beautiful collection of memories and have gratitude for the experience? Just because it isn't now doesn't lessen its truth then. Can't such things be gifts that we take with us, wherever we go?

Another possible box I've heard is "I've always thought you were like two peas in a pod." When I heard this about Brian and me, it seemed to point to the belief that because we were now divorcing, we must've never been really close to begin with—and that the person felt they'd been mistaken about our being so close before. Maybe that is my own perception and wasn't the meaning intended by the person who said that. To me, it could also point to a larger belief of "it was never meant to be." Perhaps it also points to a belief that if someone is getting a divorce, "it must've never been very good to begin with."

To me, all these beliefs are just that: beliefs. And you know what? We can *choose* our beliefs. They mean nothing to anyone who doesn't believe them. I see them as possible judgments or boxes about Brian's and my relationship that no one outside our relationship could accurately make—nor could anyone else really know about our relationship. For me, our relationship has been a beautiful, raw, enjoyable, sorrowful, and successful journey of finding out what love is. And hey, since I was there the whole time, I'm going to go with that! I'm so thankful that Brian was the man with whom I could find this. He is such a lovely, wonderful, and amazing person. It could be that judgments people make about others' "failed" relationships are ways of saying to themselves, "This is different than what I have, so that isn't going to happen to me." But, how is anything a failure, if you're learning?

We may seek a certain mental construct or societal/social structure. I think of these as replacements for actually addressing and expressing needs. We often need and want something from someone else, but instead of making that known and asking for what we need or want, we do nothing. If we are married or living with someone, for instance, we may think that within that structure we will actually have our needs met. So we don't look at our needs and wants, or talk about them. And we may find that often within some of these structures, we still will not have our needs met—and we may become frustrated, unsatisfied, or disenchanted.

A very wise young person wanted to know how people could go from wanting to be together forever to never wanting to see each other again. It does seem unnatural, doesn't it? Why one extreme or the other? I think it has to do with boxes, fear, and protecting oneself. It doesn't have to be all or nothing. It can be a platonic and loving friendship. It might take some inner work and counseling, but I think everyone is capable of this—*if* they truly want it. I think this extreme pendulum swing can also have to do with idyllic love. I think idyllic love is not real love, but something that exists only in our minds. So when we stop "seeing" our vision in the outer circumstances, *that* love disappears from the person we attached it to in the first place. Then we may try to find someone else to fit our ideal, and try to create it again.

I often think of the saying "nothing has any meaning, save the meaning I give it." Things don't have to be a certain way. Humans have given various meanings to various things throughout history—including marriage. There are times in human history and in various cultures where gender and the number of people within a marriage were not the focus. There were times and places where unions were a very transient affair, like a flowing river.[2] Nothing has to mean what it means to you unless you want it to. Nothing has to have the same meaning to you as it has for the mainstream or the majority of people. I can choose each and every day whether, for instance, my child is being "messy" or "carefree." The words I choose in my mind to describe my child, events, and people have bearing on how I *feel*. If I can choose differently, why wouldn't I? Then I can respond to people differently and that changes everything for the better. If I can feel differently (better), why wouldn't I? My brain needs to work for me, not the other way around. It is *my* brain; I do not belong to it. I have the power to change how I feel by changing the way I think and what I believe. As I changed myself, the world around me seemed to change right along with me.

Another way I've thought about things is to understand and accept the ways friends in my life have sometimes come and gone. I've also gone from their lives, I suppose. I can look back and see that we learn and grow from the sharing we engage in and then, eventually, it seems the exchange winds down. We learn and grow from each other all that we can. We always wish each other well, and still we may drift apart peacefully and quietly. This is a beautiful process among humans. I'm not saying there can be no lifelong friendships. It is just that there is a beauty about accepting and loving what is, while you

---

[2] Stephanie Coontz, *Marriage, a History: How Love Conquered Marriage* (New York, Penguin Books, 2006).

have it, and then feeling gratitude and acceptance once it passes. I've often thought that marriages or partnerships between adults could have the same freedom and acceptance for dissolution or evolution.

I discovered that words like *boyfriend* or *husband*, are just not words or concepts I want to subscribe to any more. I'm not saying that I won't have a life/learning partner, or even someone I may marry, but I would rather call him by his name. When I was thinking about the concept of a boyfriend or husband, I realized that it felt like I was talking about a cardboard cutout! Like this person would perform *these* functions and have *these* qualities, and we would have *this* arrangement, etc. I didn't like that at all. People are people, and they each have their own unique contributions and ways to be in the world. I think that instead of thinking about a structure or function, I will think about the person. Am I learning, growing, enjoying, and attracted to this person? That is what I want to focus on and this allows me to drop the feeling of needing some kind of commitment from him. That seems to go along with the idea of trying to "fit" someone to a structure I have in my mind—probably idyllic love. It feels SO GOOD to let go of that! I have cried so many times, just from feeling such relief about all of this. For me, it requires an understanding and a belief in abundance, and carrying and feeling that within romantic relationships. I've felt abundance in many areas of my life (and I want to feel that, instead of scarcity), so now I am carrying my belief and feeling of abundance to my romantic relationships. That feels so good. It was a difficult frontier and it took what felt like forever! *But* I am glad to experience this, rather than not, and I am so thankful to all of my friends for helping me with this development!

Some people think that things should be forever. I think that is a way to hang onto a false sense of security. There is no such thing as security. We may always be trying hard to "make" something that resembles security, but it is not a real thing. No matter how long we've been married, where we live, or how much money we have, we can never be truly secure.

Considering other possible boxes or judgments, some people might ask how I could be so selfish—well, OK, I've even asked myself this, although I don't truly believe that is what I am. To this, I would respond by saying that I felt so much gratitude for my life, even before Brian and I separated. I was happy. I just had a sense that there was more to learn and that I could grow in so many more ways. I needed to see what *I* was made of. I needed to see if I could take care of my own problems and issues that would arise. I also needed to learn how to ask for help if I needed it. How could I do that if there was "built-in" help? I wanted to see if I could provide for my own needs. There were so many things I wanted to know for myself, about myself—and about life.

Some people might ask, "How could you 'throw away' so many years?" I've heard that one in movies. My response to that would be that this is a belief about the situation and about relationships. To me, I'm not throwing away anything. I feel immense gratitude for the contributions Brian has made to my life and for all I have learned.

Nothing has been thrown away, in my eyes. I have made great use of the time we had together and I've taken with me all the love that we gave each other over those 17-plus years. Rebecca Lammersen, in her article "How to Have a Loving Divorce," states, "Divorce is not the end of love, it is the cessation of a pledged definition. We redefined our bond."[3] The belief some people have about "throwing it all away" could also be rooted in a sense of scarcity: the belief that there may never be anyone else to love or to be loved by. There are seven billion people on the planet. I don't think that is a problem!

---

[3]   Rebecca Lammersen, "How to Have a Loving Divorce," *elephant*, August 11, 2012, www.elephantjournal.com/2012/08/how-to-have-a-loving-divorce/.

# BOUNDARIES

*Reology offers us a new way of using words . . .*
*helping us understand that each and every*
*person is only telling us about their individual*
*perceptions—they are not telling us about us.*[1]
*~Jake and Hannah Eagle*

I'd like to share with you the concepts and process-es that have helped me with boundaries. I think of a boundary as a place where one person ends and another person begins—nothing too scary. We live in a world of individual perceptions only, and all perception is subjec-tive. No perception is more valid than another, and yet we often behave and believe otherwise.[2] If we view our own perspectives as more valid than another's, whether an individual's or a group's, we may sometimes feel we have the right to impose our will on another. This type of

[1]   Jake and Hannah Eagle, *Why Smart People Struggle to Be Happy*, 18.

[2]   Jake and Hannah Eagle, Reology.org.

behavior in humans, which is a subtle form of violence, can eventually lead to physical violence and even war. If we feel another's perspective is more valid than our own, we may follow them and even see them as something of a parental figure. True, we need to share and learn as much as we can from each other and the world; and the more open we are to others, the more open they will be to us. We need each other and each other's perspectives. But to replace our own inner authority with another person's perception (authority) about us is not a sign of a healthy boundary.

As children, we tend to deify our parents because we do not have our own strong sense of inner authority. We may think these authority figures' actions toward us determine "how good enough" or "not good enough" we are. We often go through adulthood with a similar sense of the world, looking to parents, bosses, or partners to tell us that we are good enough. That is perpetuated by our culture's way of enforcing and promoting conformity and following orders; people most often aren't supported in developing a healthy sense of autonomy or a strong inner authority, either by parents, schools, doctors, or institutions. These figures in our lives, while we are growing up, are most often teaching us to look outside ourselves for cues to dictate our next action, feeling, or choice. They tell us what to do and they often demand that we follow orders, without question. This is teaching us to look outside ourselves to "define" ourselves. This is not teaching us to listen to and develop our own inner authority—to listen to ourselves and decide for ourselves that we are good enough. It does not teach us to look to ourselves for guidance in making choices, and to honor our feelings, desires, and thoughts as being as equally valid as another's.

One valuable lesson I learned has to do with both valuing another's perception equally, and giving and receiving freely. These things are very important to me. I was making love and my partner made a very nice comment about my body. Well, you might imagine my discomfort—since I was not in love with my body at that point. The next day, I thought about why I could not receive this compliment freely. If I wanted to learn to give and receive freely, certainly receiving was part of that exchange, or circle. So I applied to this situation what I'd learned about perception. His perception of my body was just that: his perception. It didn't judge my body as far as the rest of the world was concerned, yet his perception is just as valid as anyone else's. Straightening these ideas out in that way allowed me to accept his loving comment and honor that it was the way he saw and experienced me; and it was a very lovely thing. I was glad that he felt that way and that he shared his perception with me. I'd learned a very difficult part of the circle of giving and receiving freely, and about perception. It was very nice to be able to accept and appreciate what he felt.

We live in a culture of judgment, either stemming from or made worse by religions characterized by judgment. I'm not talking about the judgments or observations made for oneself, which can help a person determine what path he or she wants to take. I'm talking about judgments made to make oneself feel better or self-righteous—and to condemn others. Judgments can also put another on a pedestal and, at the same time, put oneself down. The only judgments that are constructive and healthy, in my opinion, are the ones that help a person determine what choices he or she wants to make in life. I think these are called "value judgments," and they are made for the sake of making choices, determining one's own path in life, and setting priorities. They aren't made to put people above or below someone else.

Another thing that was so incredibly important for me to understand is that no one is more or less than anyone else. You might ponder, for a moment, that one cannot feel "better" than some people without also feeling "less" than other people. These are opposite sides of the same painful coin, and it will cause pain until it has been tossed. For me, tossing this coin involved my internalizing that I'm no more and no less than anyone else. I started in an unusual place. I looked at other creatures on Earth. Do we say things like "that duck is just not 'duck enough'"? Do we put down any other creature? Why on earth would we put down humans—ourselves? If a duck is born with a physical difference in comparison to other ducks, I would look at it and think to myself, "That duck is getting along in the world in the best way it can." I'd look at it with acceptance and compassion. If we humans are born with physical differences compared to the majority of humans, we would do the same thing: We would get along in the world in the best way we could.

People have different strengths and capacities, not all of which are celebrated by society but are no less valuable than other strengths and capacities. True, we may need to find how our strengths and capacities enrich our lives and the lives of others—how we "fit" them into the world—but they are equally valuable because they all contribute to the experience of human existence.

I think we must also look at humans compassionately when it comes to emotional, physical, and psychological wounds and trauma, which we all have likely sustained. All trauma, including something as common as the trauma we often refer to as male infant circumcision, negatively affects different areas of the brain and how well these areas communicate, or don't communicate, with one another. Trauma (and neglect alike) greatly impacts a person's ability to connect with himself or herself, others, and the environment. Most of these can be wounds that we are largely unaware of—"invisible"—but that affect our daily lives and how well we function, nonetheless. I think of these as varying degrees of health. There are no people better than or less than others, there are just varying degrees of physical, emotional, psychological, and spiritual health among people. As children, we humans don't get to choose what emotional, psychological, physical, and spiritual hurts are imposed on us by our parents, siblings, schools, medical establishments, churches, and the larger society (although some mystics may argue this point). We are given these things to deal with as best we can. Most of these things we can heal from, yes, through experience, love, focus, and effort. I think people deserve to be viewed with compassion and understanding because we all have our struggles, blind spots, and baggage, in addition to our positive aspects.

It is worth mentioning that a 35-year-old adult is considered by many psychologists to be an "old child" developmentally. We are all growing and changing all the time—but now, as adults, it is happening more on the inside than the outside. I think we humans don't realize this because of the visual "permanence" of adulthood. A friend of mine sometimes uses the quote "we are growing from womb to tomb," and she chooses not to use the term *grown-up* because it implies a false completion of maturity. We're not doing ourselves or anyone else any favors by putting ourselves down because we aren't living up to so many arbitrarily chosen standards. We are developing and evolving over our entire lives. It is my hope that we are healing throughout our lives as well. Where we are with our personal growth and healing is very individual. To look to others, expecting them to be a certain way or be capable of certain things, is really not giving oneself room to see who they are. It is us looking for what we want to see or not see—it isn't giving space for who the person actually is. I think what we might want someone to be capable of, in comparison to what they actually *are* capable of, is really indicative of our own level of subscription to arbitrarily chosen ideals—it has little or nothing to do with the other person!

Several years ago I realized that I was responsible for all of my own feelings—that no one else was. For instance, no one could *make* me angry; this reaction was a result of the way I was thinking about a situation or an interaction was triggering some past hurt that I needed to examine and heal from. This was one of the most powerful realizations I have ever made, and it began to change my life for the better, immediately. Besides beginning to use my reactions to things as indicators of something that needed to be addressed within me, I owned my power and I was realizing and beginning to assert healthier boundaries.

One thing I decided a few years ago was that I would no longer plug into roles. I was Lynda the neighbor, wife, sister, auntie, mother, daughter, etc. I was just so sick of all these different roles. I decided that I would just be Lynda, the generally loving and supportive person that I am—and that was all. If people didn't like me, I decided that was OK. No more donning roles. I still did loving, kind, and helpful things. That part of me didn't go away, because that is who I am. I was still able to be a good mother and more. I think roles are things people hide behind so they don't have to interact directly with others. Not only that, roles take a lot of energy! You know what? No one even seemed to notice that I was just being myself. People seemed to like it and so did I. I felt great being liked and loved just for being myself! I also stopped wearing makeup and jewelry years ago, and people still liked me after that too. I have found it feels wonderful to stop hiding behind roles and what felt like fake looks. It helped me to love myself more and to strengthen my inner authority—something that is so important to asserting boundaries.

I did not have healthy boundaries with either of my parents, and I have found that until or unless I changed that I would not be able to have healthy boundaries with anyone. It all begins with our parents. The quality of the dynamic I had with everyone in my life reflected the quality of the dynamic I had with my parents. Once my father died, I became aware of the level of unhealth that existed in my life regarding boundaries. I processed what I needed to, about him, after he died. One night I "had it out" with him, even though he was obviously not there to hear it. It helped me to be able to assert my boundary, express my anger, and process everything I needed to process. Once I was free of him and what felt like his hold on my life, I felt so good. I knew there was no way I would wait until my mother passed away to be free of what felt like her unhealthy hold on my life. I wasn't going to let another minute pass without starting my work on freeing myself of our unhealthy dynamic.

My mother is an enabler, and I felt as though she treated me like property when I was young. (She was probably treated like she was property when she was young, too.) I felt like my mother's caregiver and caregiver to her children, my younger siblings. I felt I needed to be everything to everyone, and I feel now, looking back, as though I was dying inside—suffocating. That's what it felt like anyway. Her neediness, which she pacified by using random threats and subtle manipulation to get what she wanted from me (and my siblings), was only made to seem more "urgent" by my father's violent, volatile, and abusive behavior. We had a live-in terrorist, and my mother seemed so powerless and needy that I always had a heightened sense of alertness and duty to everyone. I don't think I ever really was able to have an actual childhood, to play and feel safe in my own home. The only times I remember feeling safe was when my father traveled on business. Fortunately, for a couple years, that was fairly regularly.

The relationship I had with my mother was extremely dysfunctional. As an adult, I became increasingly uncomfortable with it. It was as though I was her mother and she was addicted to being able to get a hold of me on the phone whenever she wanted me. She would call repeatedly, and if I didn't answer, then she'd call Brian's phone to see if she could get me that way. When I didn't answer, I felt guilty. I began to feel like a sitting duck. Upon hearing the phone ring, I thought, "What will she take from me this time?" Just writing this brings up the emotional memory of what that felt like. It was awful.

I needed to figure out how to fix this. I wouldn't live with this any longer. My mother was sixty-eight years old at that point, and if she hadn't grown up yet, it probably wasn't going to happen—and I certainly wasn't going to allow the effort I put into parenting her to take up any more of my life. I needed to be able to open up to heal, and I couldn't do that when I felt so unsafe because of her calling me all the time. I felt so guilt-ridden and defenseless over it. I really had no boundaries when it came to my mother. Our relationship was so dysfunctional. I decided I would tell her that I needed time without her calling me. I let her know that I had anger I needed to work out, among other things. At first, I think she was angry, but she left me alone. I needed her to grow up and leave me alone. I was so guilt-ridden over this decision that I actually needed to get confirmation from my sisters and brother that this was OK to do. They supported me.

During the time I didn't have contact with my mother I discovered some experiences from childhood that I'd repressed. They were experiences that I'd attributed to her. I was able to address and express them, mourn, and then let them go. The anger that I'd had toward my mother evaporated. I was really relieved. I'd wanted to be able to let go of that for probably eight months, and I was so glad to get to the bottom of what that was. I'd been so puzzled over what it had to do with.

After that, things got better and better. The longer I lived on my own, the healthier I became and my sense of self became stronger. I was taking my power back all over the place. Judgments I'd perceived that others had toward me were completely dissolving and I was feeling safer and safer just being me. I trusted myself more and more and I was becoming increasingly comfortable in my own skin.

I remember seeing my mother unexpectedly at the farmers' market one day. I just felt like saying "hi," giving her a hug, and then moving on with what I was doing. I felt uncomfortable and she started following me and it just didn't seem good. I felt as though I was fleeing and she probably felt abandoned. It was not a very good feeling. Then, a couple of weeks later, I saw her again at the farmers' market. I don't know what changed, but this time I felt like she was just another person. I mean, she was my mother, but that was it. She paid for something for me, which is maybe a norm for mothers, but definitely a norm for my mother. I just decided that I wasn't going to feel guilty about anything and that her decision to buy me something was just that—*her* decision. I owed her nothing. I didn't ask her to do that. I was getting ready to pay and she just wiggled in and paid. I just finally had reached the point where I internalized that I owed her nothing. Her decisions were hers and my decisions were mine and we could each do what we wanted to do. She was my mother, she chose to have me. I didn't ask to be her daughter, I didn't ask to be born even—that I can recall. That is it. There was nothing unpleasant about seeing her that day. I thanked her for buying my apples, gave her a hug, and we talked briefly as we walked to my car. It was nice that I didn't discourage her from buying the apples, as I might have done before. It was the beginning of freedom and it was great. The long-sought-after boundary was finally in place.

A few weeks later my mother and I had lunch together. Partway through the meal, she was trying to tell me to do something to help one of my siblings feel satisfied with a decision he'd made. I calmly let her know that I would do that if it worked for me and if I felt a genuine desire to do so, but that making sure my brother was happy with a decision he'd made for himself was not my responsibility. That felt so good and we had a nice lunch together. A few weeks after that, my sister and I took my mother out for lunch for her 70th birthday. It felt so good to see her and I felt genuine love and compassion for her, free of any feelings of obligation or unpleasant feelings of guilt. It was wonderful. I'm truly happy to talk to her on the phone now, and I ask her if it is OK with her before I talk to her about personal things that are going on with me and that may be causing me some inner conflict. I feel as though we are done "using" each other and now we can just have a nice relationship. It feels *so good*! I'm both relieved and grateful that our relationship can be joyful and healthy! This is my perception of our relationship, anyway.

Asserting a healthy boundary with my mother allowed me to feel genuine compassion for her, rather than obligated or feigned compassion. It feels so good to really feel love for my mother, without there being negative feelings mixed in with it.

It is my understanding that the health of a person's current relationships roughly resembles the degree of health of the relationships they have or had with their own parents. Since the relationships with our parents are the very first and longest relationships we know, it makes perfect sense to me that all other relationships will carry a similar or identical dynamic. Basically, I feel that the health of my relationship with Brian loosely reflected the health of the relationships I had with my parents. I think since I was able to grow through some of the dysfunction and make important psychological and emotional connections regarding my parents, I'm much more capable of having relationships that reflect greater health and that are more functional now.

It has been a good thing for me to realize early on that my children don't owe me; and later, to realize that I don't owe my parents. I feel that if I'm actually taking responsibility for my choices and not playing the victim, I would not feel that my children owe me. I chose to have children; they didn't just happen to me. We are raising them to the best of our ability. Does this mean they somehow owe us something? I don't think so. For all the good we provide them, we provide them an equal amount of woes and wounds because we ourselves are wounded and imperfect. My children have taught me so much and have changed my life for the better. Their fresh eyes have shed light on life for me in ways I never could have imagined, and I'm truly grateful. They have graced my life. For me, the "exchange" within the parent-child relationship is pretty even. And even if it weren't, in my case it was my choice to have my children, more than it was their choice to be born.

A particular therapy that helped me during my healing process is EMDR. It stands for "eye movement desensitization reprocessing." It has about a twenty-year history, and it was so beneficial for me in healing my trauma. Words cannot accurately describe how healing this therapy was. Unprocessed trauma, as I understand it, is indicated by anxiety, controlling behaviors, panic attacks, and/or PTS (post-traumatic stress). I found a counselor in my area who has, at minimum, EMDR–Part 2 training, which, I have been told, is a good level of qualification to seek in a counselor. If I had known ahead of time how draining this therapy is, I would have allowed myself some time to rest afterward. I had a headache and felt as though I was healing from minor surgery for a couple of days.

This last thing I want to mention about boundaries might sound rather odd. I discovered this spontaneously one day, and then a year or so later, discovered it was something others had identified too. It is called "primal (scream) therapy"[3] and was discovered and developed by psychologist Arthur Janov. As I understand it, it is a therapy in which unprocessed trauma or pain is released through a primal scream, which creates space within for integration of the senses and emotions. I've only done this a handful of times, and on my own, but it has always been an amazingly profound experience for me. It is helpful because, in my experience, it takes the pain of the past and releases it into the present—allowing it to be and giving space to all that I felt but had never given space to (permission to express) before. I found that it not only helped me to process pain, sadness, and anger, it helped me to assert boundaries with both my mother and my father (who was deceased at the time). This primal experience allowed me to claim all that I was and have felt, but was never allowed to experience for lack of feeling powerful and safe. Not only was it a release and process of pain, it was like claiming my space for who I was, and allowing my feelings to be in the world. I was claiming adequate "space" for myself in the world, for the first time—space for *all* aspects of myself.

---

[3]   www.primaltherapy.com/what-is-primal-therapy.php

# What Might a Healthy Romantic Relationship Look Like?

*Out beyond ideas of wrongdoing and rightdoing,*
*there is a field. I'll meet you there.[1] ~Rumi*

What might a healthy romantic relationship look like? To be perfectly honest, I don't really know that for myself yet. I think all of my relationships are egalitarian relationships now, and that is what I want, for sure. I think that the healthier I become, the healthier my relationships will be—all of them, not only the romantic ones. I think I will even be attracted to healthier people. I've removed many "crutches" from my life, things that were enabling me to hold down emotional baggage. I gave up sex (and orgasm) for enough time to find and deal with what was underneath that addiction. Now I find that it is no longer an addiction. That is awesome!

---

[1] http://www.worldprayers.org/archive/prayers/meditations/out_beyond_ideas_of_wrong.html

About a month into my vow of celibacy, I stopped con-
suming chocolate (temporarily—come on, I'm not *that*
crazy!), and a month after that, I removed Facebook from
my life. Sex, chocolate, and social media were things that
were distracting me and/or releasing chemicals and hormones into my body that were making me feel good and
holding down unprocessed emotional baggage.

I also kicked monogamy's ass. What do I mean by
this? Well, I got over female sexual oppression. In our
culture and in many other cultures, I think this is co-
vertly, and sometimes overtly, shoved down virtually
every female's throat. It's also just something made up,
in my opinion, and it tends to influence women to feel
uncomfortable and bad about their sexuality and themselves—unless they are adhering to specific guidelines
for expressing their sexuality. Maybe the guidelines for
"approved" expressions of sexuality for women would be
expressions within marriage or a committed relationship.
I don't think that "prescribed" sexuality is healthy sexuality, necessarily. I think healthy sexuality is individual
to each person, and it is something one *chooses* for oneself based on what feels best to the individual. I can now
choose what feels best to me and I'm in the process of fig-
uring out what that is. I really had to let go of what society,
or even my neighbor, might think if I were to engage in
sexual expression freely. It was difficult at first because I
was afraid of being judged. That lasted about two weeks
and I worked through it. Now, to me, possible judgment
about my sexual expression is all just cultural or individual opinion and it has no power over me anymore.

When I was married I felt like I *needed* monogamy in order to feel OK. I've since opened up to the ideas of open marriages/relationships and polyamory. That doesn't mean I will choose these things now or choose them long term. It just means that now I can actually make the choice of monogamy, should I choose it—and not just accept it out of necessity because I feel as though I would fall apart if I didn't have it. This feels incredibly freeing and so much healthier.

So now I feel like I can really *choose* all these things: monogamy, chocolate, sex, romantic relationships, Facebook, etc. I don't *need* them to the point of creating unhealthy patterns and disordered priorities in my life. They aren't ruling my life. I'm already well on my way to creating much healthier relationships now that I have worked on, and continue to work on, myself. Another really great thing is that I can be without a partner and enjoy it! This means that I will enter into relationships that feel good to me. I won't enter into a relationship because I need to have a relationship to avoid the fear and discomfort of being on my own.

I think that a healthy relationship would be one in which the partners would each have their own rich, full life, independent of the other's life but intertwining and sharing in mutually agreeable ways. I think the partners would support one another in ways they agreed upon, but these ways would be ever-evolving and open for re-evaluation. These are just my ideas.

As I said before, it is one thing to make a request and quite another to make demands or use manipulation to get what we want. Asking to have a need met is very different than making demands and using coercion or more subtle forms of manipulation to get those needs met. Sometimes we may not even conceptualize our needs. Sometimes they are just unpleasant feelings that we want to make "go away," and we simply do whatever the moment calls for to make that happen. I think it is important and healthy to conceptualize a need and then ask for help from others to meet those needs.

I think the relationship Brian and I have is becoming healthier all the time. We are able to be more fully ourselves because our lives are not so intertwined. We are able to be more unconditionally supportive of each other. For instance, last year I thought Brian was asking me out to lunch. I said that it would be great and that I'd really like to make out because I'd been celibate for a long time (it seemed long to me by the time the vow was over!). I then realized he was responding to an earlier question about a lunchtime arrangement we had made about the children, and he wasn't asking me to lunch. He confirmed that misunderstanding and then let me know that he didn't feel like making out and he was sorry about that. I said, "OK." Then I thought about it for a bit and wondered why he would feel sorry for his feelings. I certainly didn't feel sorry for mine and I was so glad to honor myself by expressing my feelings. I told him that I didn't think he needed to be sorry for his feelings. They were his feelings and he needed to honor them. He agreed and we moved on happily from there. I really love that we can express ourselves honestly and that it is OK. What we feel deserves respect and honor, and we can express it, but if our feelings don't match up, then that is OK and we don't need to take it personally.

Another interesting interaction that took place was when I felt a slight shift in Brian's level of availability (which I realized was good for me and forced me to, say, fix my own printer). I suspected he was seeing or sleeping with someone. I asked him one evening when he came over. He said yes, he was getting close to sleeping with someone. I said, "Oh, OK," and I put my hand on his shoulder and smiled. I said that I didn't want there to be any reason to feel secretive. I was getting ready for bed at that point, so I went into the bathroom to brush my teeth and when I saw myself in the mirror, I had a huge smile on my face. I was thinking, "Oh, he's so sweet!" I liked that I felt genuine happiness for him about his meeting his needs and doing what he felt drawn to do.

I slept well that night. The next morning, I looked for discomfort within myself about the situation. I could scarcely believe that within our culture, I could feel such happiness about a situation such as this! I felt myself seemingly differing from the mainstream in a new way. I felt like a weirdo and I was a bit uncomfortable for a couple of hours, as I settled into what seemed to be a drastically unique experience and perspective. Fortunately, I have some very loving friends who each told me that this was a very good thing and that I was not a weirdo! I was relieved to have their support. Phew! For whatever reason, it can take me a little time to adjust to becoming more myself, especially if it makes me feel so different from my culture and family. Later that day, I felt a bit of sadness about the possibility of my friendship with Brian becoming less than what it had been, due to his getting close to someone else. I mentioned something about that to him later that afternoon. It was a good conversation and I felt better just having shared my feelings. I'm so grateful that he was willing to listen.

Something that helps me is the idea that we all deserve to be loved and accepted for all of who we are, not just the aspects that are deemed approved or valuable by society or others. We are all products of our unhealthy culture and I think we are all complicit to the extent in which we participate and "go along" with our societal systems and behaviors that are hurtful to each other and that are ignorant of human needs. In fact, I think until we accept an aspect of ourselves that we don't like, so much of our energy goes into resisting it and feeling loathsome over it. There just isn't as much energy available to use to actually change what we want to change about ourselves. I think that humans have varying degrees of what each can hold within one's awareness and consciousness at a time. We have a limited amount of focus and energy to apply to our lives each day. I think it is wise to actively choose what we want to put our focus and energy on. I think it is also wise to be compassionate toward others, whose focus and range of awareness is being directed toward something we may not understand; they may not have the emotional or mental "space" to address something we might think would be more important or beneficial. If we talk to others compassionately we can often find out where they are, so that we can better support them regarding their interests and struggles. The idea of pushing someone to do what seems like a better alternative is really not helpful to a person's process. We don't know where another person is and what they might need.

It is important for me to accept that no one is perfect and everyone I meet will have issues. I have issues that I hope someone will accept—and help me with my own awareness, growth, and acceptance of these issues. I have issues of which I'm both aware and unaware. I hope to find someone with whom I can experience a mutually agreeable, give-and-take relationship—one in which we both feel comfortable asking for and giving help to meet each other's needs. If I can honor all that I am, I think it will help me to honor all that someone else is, too.

Remember the observer within that I spoke about? I have realized that this inner observer can also love me the way I want to be loved. I know it sounds strange—but really, this inner observer loves me just the way I want to be loved and has "filled my cup" completely. There is such healing in that. I've heard the idea "if you don't love yourself, how is anyone else supposed to love you?" I think this speaks volumes. There is such healing and fulfillment in loving myself. Now I feel as though I may be able to enjoy the ways that someone else can love me, without hoping that his love will fit the certain love-shaped void I once had within me. I want to be vulnerable and honest in all of my relationships. I would also like to be in the moment, and defining a relationship in some way is not something I'm interested in, at least not presently.

All the connections I have, whether with friends, family, or neighbors, are all relationships. There are just varying degrees and aspects of sharing that take place within those relationships. I don't see why a relationship, characterized by sexual sharing, needs some special definition or arrangement. Why put a structure to something that is free, spontaneous, authentic, and open to how the parties really feel, from one moment to the next? That seems counterintuitive, an oxymoron, if you will. It seems that putting a structure of some kind, a definition, into a relationship could affect the authenticity and organic development of that experience. Needing to project a relationship structure into the future can have to do with fear, I think, and allaying certain unsettling feelings within oneself.

I'd found myself within a hypnotic and subtle habit of projecting a structure into a relationship, which is a common power struggle between romantic/dating partners. A friend and I were pondering things one day and I noticed how it seems that often women tend to control sex, and she noticed how it seems men often tend to control relationship status. It seems the two parties sometimes use these aspects as power plays in relationships—maybe even as currency, I don't know. I don't know how or if this dynamic plays out in gay and lesbian relationships, as I'm heterosexual, but I imagine it likely would. I wanted to be able to let go of the limiting attachment to having a (possible) long-term relationship with my sexual partner. I wanted to be able to live in the moment and enjoy things as they were. I think fear was making me want to project a possible long-term relationship into the future.

I think each one of us has within just what we need, all the time; we just might not know it or feel it. Being in the moment and enjoying my relationships, whatever types of sharing they consist of, feels really good to me now that I'm more capable of doing that. Every interaction feels like such a gift, and I feel truly grateful to honor others and be honored by others.

We all want to belong, I think—to be accepted. So opening up and being honest about what I feel, what I like, and what I want has been difficult, since many of these realizations tend to leave me feeling quite the minority. I must say, at the same time that I feel like an odd person, I feel really good in embracing who I am. I feel happy about being myself. It has taken me a long time and much effort to weed through the things that were imposed on me and to see and feel what it is that is underneath—what it is that I actually feel, like, and want. I remember when I felt as though I didn't have the faintest clue what it was that I actually felt, liked, and wanted! That felt like such a sad place to be. It felt like I didn't know who I was. I remember feeling such disbelief when I came to the realization that I knew very little about myself. I really do feel that having a healthy relationship with oneself lends itself to having healthy relationships with others.

# To Each, His or Her Own Unique Journey

*If a man does not keep pace with his companions,*
*perhaps it is because he hears a different drummer.*
*Let him step to the music which he hears,*
*however measured or far away.[1]*
*~Henry David Thoreau*

After about a year of living apart, Brian met some-one. He altered his boundaries very quickly. It was difficult, but it was for the best. One thing that was really not OK with me was that, at first, he would just say he was going out of town, without really talking to the children and me about it. He was, in my eyes, acting as though his feelings, wants, and needs were somehow more important than ours. That is not reality. He was essentially demanding when I would be 100 percent responsible for our children, at his whim.

---

[1] Henry David Thoreau, *Walden* (Boston, Ticknor and Fields, 1854).

That did not bode well for me for a couple reasons. One, because we both agreed not to make the children go from house to house on our schedule. This meant that they were with me most of the time. I'm OK with that. I love them and I don't want to shuffle them back and forth, if they don't want to be shuffled. This also meant that just because they are with me most of the time, I'm not the default responsible parent. Brian is just as responsible for them as I am, and the children need him to be available to them too. He had some beliefs, which he shared with me, that were leading him to feel like he was privileged and had more freedom than I did. He felt that because he'd worked so hard, he got to do whatever he wanted and I just had to deal with it. Brian was under the illusion that he'd worked harder and had contributed more to the family. He felt that the child support was covering all the children's expenses and that this meant he could just leave when he wanted. That was not true. Neither had he contributed more to our family, nor was the child support covering all the children's expenses.

To be fair, I'd not understood that my prior contributions to our family, as a stay-at-home parent, were equally valuable, even though I knew I'd poured my blood, sweat, and tears into our family. I'm sure that my false belief that my contributions were less valuable made room for his false belief that his contributions were more valuable. The belief I had has a lot to do with the fact that the nurturing, research, and work that goes into caring for children and a household is just not compensated for in dollars and cents. The tangible value is not there so there's no easy way of measuring these contributions. I feel like now that I'm working and know what both types of contributions feel like (because I make both everyday), I can say from experience that nurturing children and taking care of a household should never be undervalued. It is hard and creative work! Because I've been able to experience both, I've been able to heal from all those years of feeling like what I was giving wasn't quite as valuable as what Brian was giving. You cannot place a dollar value on what a caregiving mother (or father) does; you can't measure it with a tape, so it is so easily dismissed as being less valuable than jobs that pay. It is not.

The other thing that made Brian's demands sting was that, as a child, I'd experienced my mother demanding that I care for my younger siblings, with not even a moment's notice or care about what I felt. I had a need for consideration that was not being met. I had a need to have my feelings, desires, and needs be treated as equally important as others' feelings, desires, and needs. This is one of the experiences I was referring to when I said that when I was a child I felt as though I was treated like property. Here it was being repeated, only this time the children were actually mine (and Brian's). But I had the same horrible feeling inside. It was awful.

One of the reasons I was having such a hard time working this out with Brian was that I believed that he was trying to exploit me. This belief was attached to my larger belief that "people were always trying to exploit me." I realized it probably came from childhood and my feeling that I was being treated like a commodity that could be used as needed. I needed to drop that belief, which is actually very victim oriented, and merge that with my understanding that people are just trying to meet their needs the very best ways they know how—period. It took away the feeling that Brian was doing something malicious to me, and brought me to a space where I could open up and talk to him without assuming he was trying to use or hurt me. How incredibly helpful to the quality of our communication! Wow, that was a really old childhood belief that was still present within me. How amazing that I'd not discovered and dealt with it sooner.

Brian and I discussed these issues and I think things are getting better. It was just a very difficult time for us—at least I know it was difficult for me. We've adjusted even more boundaries. I've decided, for myself, that I will leave my home every other weekend and Brian can come here to be with the children—or he can ask them to come to his house. I wanted to remove myself from the situation, so the three of them have the room to work out the sleeping arrangements for themselves. If one or both of the children miss me, I can come by and pick one or both of them up for a bit and we can do something together. It is not that I want to get away from them—I just want time to myself (a slightly different focus, I think).

For a variety of reasons, I feel I needed time to myself and I think Brian and the children also needed more options and independence in working out something that worked for all of them regarding the weekends he would be with them. We talked about it before making the decision to do this. We addressed some concerns so that it would work OK for all of us. This arrangement helps me to have a life and identity of my own, separate from that of a mother, which I think helps me to be a better mother. I don't want my children to feel responsible for my personal sense of self, and having a more balanced sense of self helps me to be a healthier individual, separate from my identity as a mother. I think I'm able to have much healthier and balanced relationships with my children. I think I can see their conflicts and needs much more objectively and balanced, instead of trying to fit those into the shape I needed them to be, as their mother. It also helps me express my needs too—which, by the way, I needed to believe were just as important as others' needs. As I was relying on motherhood as part of my identity, part of the unbalanced dynamic was to care for my children and to not ask for what I needed. It tended to feel a bit self-effacing and I don't think that was good for them or me. I think the children see a change in me and I think they feel it is positive. Also, this way they get to spend even more regular time with their father, which is very important. Certainly, the ways in which we have arranged the children's time with their father always seems to be evolving. This makes sense because sometimes I'll have a strong need, one or both of the children will have a strong need, or Brian will have a strong need; and we all need to be able to express those needs, and support each other as well as we can. I like that nothing is in stone and we can all talk about our needs and address them, as we go.

In breaking away as an individual even more, it was difficult coming to terms with the fact that I'm the only one who can choose what is OK for me. It was difficult to accept the power to choose and to have inner authority over whether or not my choices, my body, and my opinions were OK. Certainly we need others' perspectives, we need to bounce ideas off one another, etc., but ultimately, what I say for me is what goes. What I say is OK for me, is OK for me. It was so strange to discover that this was one of the difficult things for me regarding being without a partner. I'd relinquished this inner authority of mine to my parents—my father—and then to Brian. Then when he really separated from me and built an identity around his new girlfriend and left this power to me, I felt an urgency to give it to someone else. I felt an urgency to give it over to another man. I didn't want it! I was afraid of it. I'd never before held that power within myself. I'd always given it over to someone else, at least to some degree. I'd never taken full responsibility for my choices and the consequences of those choices. Once I made this intellectual connection about my fear, I was able to see that I would prefer to have all the say over my own life and choices. Why would I ever want to give that power away? What a great thing to discover and not just give over to someone else! Wow!

Soon after this realization, I'd felt myself falling into that old pattern and I took charge of it and pressed "pause." I'd felt myself falling for someone and was so conflicted about it because I noticed feeling that what this person felt and thought about me mattered more to me than what I felt and thought about myself. That did not feel healthy or OK with me. It was seductive, yes, but it also caused pain and gave so much power to this other person—who was, indeed, just another person, like me! (Weirdness abounds sometimes!) Not only was this person just another person, like me, he was not going to have to live with the consequences of my choices, beliefs, and feelings about myself. Of course not. I was the one who would live with the consequences of my choices, beliefs, and feelings about me, as these things make up my own internal reality. Why on earth should anyone else be given power over me in these ways? It is ridiculous to think about. I would imagine this was leftover from childhood, and yet again, since my life had been such that I'd not needed to or chosen to face this, this was the first time it had come to light for me.

# MAKING FRIENDS
# WITH NEEDS

*And if you make this music for the human needs
you have within yourself, then you do it for all
humans who need the same things. Ultimately,
you enrich humanity with the profound
expression of these feelings..[1] ~Billy Joel*

As humans, we all have needs, and as one of my dear friends says, "Needs are what connect us all as humans." I really like this idea, as it helps me to better "make friends" with needs, because human connection is so important to me. A while ago, I made a list of human needs (needs I could identify) and entitled it "Human Needs Are Beautiful." It was one of my first steps toward actively working on accepting all of my own needs, some of the things that nurture me as a human being. This is what it said and I tried to make my list look pretty:

[1]   Billy Joel, commencement speech, Berklee College of Music, May 1993.

Physical Contact ~ Friends ~ Healthy Food ~ Clean Water ~ Play ~ Intellectual Stimulation ~ Love ~ Sex ~ Nature ~ Exercise ~ New Experiences ~ New Ideas ~ Honor of Other Forms of Life ~ Sleep ~ Clean Air ~ Creativity Outlet~ Art ~ Hygiene ~ Affection ~ Warmth ~ Acceptance ~ Human Connection ~ Open Communication ~ Support ~ Collaboration ~ Empathy ~ Help ~ Rest ~ Honoring My Body ~ Honoring Others

If you made a list of human needs, maybe it would look quite different from mine. I'm sure there are so many needs I haven't thought of and each person's list would probably look at least a little bit different. I'd started to address my issue with needs because, based on a suggestion from a dear friend, I read about my personality type in the Enneagram. The Enneagram, as I understand it, is a personality typing system that is thought to be from the ancient Sufi religion. Each personality type is based on a person's overall experience as a child. One of the main lessons for my personality type is to learn that my needs are OK. I have found that this was, indeed, truly a sore spot with me.

I've been uncomfortable with others' needs—probably because I was uncomfortable with my own needs. This has not been a good feeling and contributed largely to my being emotionally unavailable in some ways. Up until very recently, my emotional unavailability was below my radar; I didn't know that I was not really giving space and honor to others' feelings and needs—at least not to the point where I was in touch with my own feelings when doing so.

When my siblings and I were young, our parents were probably most concerned about meeting their own needs, not about meeting ours. Even if they tried really hard to meet our needs and were healthy enough to do so, they'd miss some—anyone would. They probably didn't know how to treat our needs and desires with equal importance to their own. It seems to me that all behaviors reflect a need that a person, of any age, is trying to meet. When a child acts out, instead of the parent trying to see if the child is hungry, tired, upset about something, or has another unmet need, often the parent tries to end the undesirable behavior as quickly as possible—as in, the parent is trying to meet his or her own need for the behavior to cease, above all. Often, this is achieved by the parent behaving punitively toward the child. Then the child learns to detest his or her own needs (and maybe even him or herself), the way the parent seems to detest the rudimentary ways in which the child is trying to express the need and ask for help to meet the need.

I think this is maybe one of the reasons my needs were so difficult for me to be OK with. Children don't often know how to say, for instance, "I'm feeling upset because I don't feel that I was being considered a moment ago." They also probably don't know how to say something like, "I'm feeling tired, hungry, and overstimulated by all the activity of the day, so I'm falling apart right now and I need your help." No, they often cry, hit a sibling, throw something, do anything they can do to express their needs and upset feelings, which may include feelings of helplessness and desperation. I think it is up to the parent to be understanding and to see that the child is not "giving them a hard time," the child is "having a hard time." Doesn't that sound like the epitome of the victim mentality, to think that a child's acting out is an intentional desire to cause disruption in one's life? Maybe this reaction to a child's rudimentary ways of expressing his or her needs is a result of the parent feeling overwhelmed and disconnected from his or her own needs.

Perhaps it is up to the parent to teach the child a language of needs, which will help them to communicate their needs more effectively. Easier said than done, right? I imagine the parent would have to "make friends" with his or her own needs and learn healthy ways to meet them, to be able to better accept their child's needs. And, the parent would have to know a language of needs and be able to model the desired or effective way of communicating and meeting needs. The parent would have to help the child identify and verbalize his or her needs by asking the child questions about how he or she is feeling. Then, the parent would put the needs into words that help the child learn how to express him or herself in a way that is easier to understand. This is no easy task, especially if the concept is so foreign.

Psychologist Marshall Rosenberg's book *Nonviolent Communication: A Language of Life* really helped me begin to learn the language of needs. He even wrote a book about parenting called *Raising Children Compassionately: Parenting the Nonviolent Communication Way.* This gem is worth a read, and I think best read immediately following the first book.

Differentiating needs from beliefs is *hugely* beneficial. We can turn concepts that are subject to interpretation into very personal beliefs. It can be difficult to examine our beliefs because we often cannot differentiate ourselves from our beliefs, as we tend to feel strongly toward them. It tends to be a scary and threatening thought because beliefs are often what we cling to in order to make sense of our world and to feel connected to it—and safe. One might consider this question: If we are unable to examine our beliefs—are not free to choose, "un-choose," or revise them—do we hold our beliefs or do our beliefs hold us?

I'm thinking of concepts like respect, honor, and consideration. For instance, I have a need for consideration. My biggest trigger, I think, is when I don't feel I'm being considered. (A trigger is a non-life threatening situation that engages a person's flight/flight response system.) Interestingly, what I believe consideration to be and what others may believe consideration to be may be very different. This was very important to learn because it helps me not to be as reactive or hostile toward a person who I feel is not checking in with me before making decisions that affect me. It also helps me not to feel as hurt. Instead of freaking out, I can just let the person know my need for consideration and what consideration means to me. Then we'll go from there. Two very wonderful and close friends helped me to realize this difference in beliefs, and I'm truly grateful. I think they deserve medals or some social recognition for their lasting and loving devotion toward me. I feel this was really such a tough and raw journey they made with me. I will be forever grateful.

Later, I realized there were even more subtle beliefs that were lying underneath that trigger. I found that I believed that if someone didn't consider me when making a decision, then they didn't feel I was competent—otherwise, why wouldn't they talk to me about a decision that may affect me or that I might want to be included in? I also believed that I must not be very important to the person—I must not really be worthy of (their) love. These underlying beliefs were really hard to face, but once I did, I threw them out. They were not true at all. How does the way that someone else processes decisions have anything to do with how competent and worthy of love I may be? That is simply preposterous! Wow, to be truly free of that cycle of pain and upset that I've experienced my whole life is truly amazing! Truly! These beliefs were so old and subtle that I'd had no idea they were there, let alone that they were the real cause of my biggest trigger—and of my intensely emotional upsets.

Now I can decide for myself, independent of another's actions, that I am competent, worthy of love, and a good person. I can know these things for myself. To me, that is an amazing personal freedom.

# ACCEPTANCE

*We do not grow absolutely, chronologically. We
grow sometimes in one dimension, and not in
another; unevenly. We grow partially. We are
relative. We are mature in one realm, childish in
another. The past, present, and future mingle and
pull us backward, forward, or fix us in the present. We are made up of layers, cells, constellations.*[1]
~ *Anaïs Nin*

I think it is beneficial and productive to accept where
you are, right now. I remember talking to Brian about
wanting to improve the quality of our communication
for our sakes and, equally importantly, for our children's
sakes. It was then that I decided to accept and appreciate
how well we were doing right then. Both of us had had
difficult childhoods and here we were, divorced and taking a long trip together, doing the very best we could. Of
course we were doing great, just how we were, right in
that very moment!

---

[1]  The Diary of Anaïs Nin Vol. 4 (1971); as quoted in Journal of
Phenomenological Psychology Vol. 15 (1984).

I understood that if we communicated negatively toward one another, it was because we were afraid and we didn't know another way to communicate and handle the situation. No one was being purposefully malicious! We just needed to learn a new way. This was such a helpful realization and it helped me to accept and love both Brian and myself even more.

It also allowed an opening for me to be able to see a way in which I was communicating passive-aggressively toward Brian. It was so sad and I felt so remorseful about having communicated with him like that, and for quite some time. It felt as though I could never make up for treating him so poorly. I learned a lot about myself and the ways I communicate with Brian—some of which are quite violent. It is subtle, but it is there and he feels it. Part of what I'd been doing was using the children's feelings as a club—as in, I was using their feelings to "gang up" on him when he wasn't doing what I wanted.

Upon coming to that realization, I was so incredulous. I felt that this was one of the cruelest and most awful things I could do. To think I'd not been able to see it until then. Unbelievable! I apologized to Brian, explained what I could now see, and then I needed to forgive myself. I talked to the children about my discovery—about how I'd sometimes abusively communicated to their father but hadn't realized it. I apologized to them too. It was such a humbling experience and it was so difficult. It is amazing to realize some of the patterns we humans get into. It may be difficult to see the true nature of some of the knee-jerk ways we handle situations. Wow—I reeled from the realization of my abusive behavior. There were *so* many tears—I felt so much sorrow for my behavior, for Brian and our children. I felt gratitude for seeing it. I felt acceptance for myself. My whole world shifted. It took some time to integrate all of this. I couldn't believe that I could behave that way and not see it—and not feel it.

We all have difficult moments communicating compassionately sometimes. Communication is difficult! We all mess up sometimes, but I think if we have the focus of loving interactions in our minds and hearts, we will quickly find a way to return to them.

There have been some situations that have been difficult, but so much has been about letting go, grieving, and accepting myself. The ways in which I do not accept myself initiate and fuel the projections I have toward Brian and a given situation. Ugh! It's not easy to see those negative qualities in myself! It's much easier for me to sacrifice him to those behaviors and traits. I just have to look back at myself and love and accept myself unconditionally. I can spend forever and a day working on each individual projection and never reach the end of the succession! I've had to go to the source of the projections: unacceptance of myself. I definitely share my feelings. It's not all about me changing and growing. But I can't make him do anything. All I can do is speak my truth, giving him the opportunity to know what is going on for me and possibly reassess, and then I need to move on and feel better. There is nothing more to it. So simply stated, yet it can be so difficult to do!

I think everyone is experiencing what they need to experience, and that helped me not to take things personally, feel resentment, or feel like belittling someone else's experience (even if just in my mind). I can never know what it is like to be in someone else's shoes. If I ever think or act as though I do, it is a boundary violation, in my opinion.

One day I found myself really frustrated with Brian over what I found to be his most dreadful quality: he has a seeming inability to take into account the many details of life and, therefore, seems to have difficulty orchestrating various events in life. It's what I'd found most frustrating about him during the time I've known him, but it was mostly subconscious for me. One event in particular, in which he was in charge on behalf of one of our children, was falling apart and I felt resentful that I had to babysit him. I was pretty angry about having to save the day. Then something happened—I made something happen. I decided to accept that "flaw" in him. I didn't want to feel angry anymore. I wanted harmony and happiness. I knew my bad feeling about him hurt our children. I knew it did and I wanted to stop it. I also accepted that I had the choice to save the day, or not. And one thing that happened, almost immediately, is that I was able to accept a negative quality within myself—the thing I hated most about myself. It turns out, it is really the same quality I disliked so much in Brian, and I think is responsible for his inability to take details into account. I tend to be rather self-absorbed, and so can he. It's my most loathsome quality, in my opinion. I think I saw that mirrored in him and I hated it.

Sure, this quality manifests in each of us differently, but I think the source is the same: being self-absorbed— at least, at times. I'd already somewhat looked at that quality within myself and seen the positive side of that shadow, the good qualities that I have that result from being self-absorbed sometimes. Accepting Brian really helped me to love myself more and to love him more too. I could then also see that this quality of self-absorption, which may contribute to his seeming inability to take logistics into account, might be the shadow side to the very quality I most admire in him: his inherent playfulness. What if his seeming inability to take into account the many details of life is the very same "flaw" that affords him the ability to be playful with our children? I love that quality in him. I've always loved it. I accept him the way he is and now my experience of him is different: it's really pleasant. This is such a gift, and it's so much more productive to take the energy I was using on feeling loathsome and use it for something else! Love and acceptance really are bigger than anything else and support such a state of happiness and contentment.

One thing that I think happens when we really dislike a quality in someone else is that we condemn them to be that way forever. Instead of seeing potential in an ever-changing, ever-evolving being, we see a judgment of "forever" and we condemn the individual to that behavior or trait for all eternity. How awful is that? It's like we've taken a quality we hate and entombed it within a living, changing being— not a fixed, inanimate object. Wow, that is really so far from the reality of any situation. What stories we create! What fiction! I think if we love and accept each other, then we can heal and grow into the highest and greatest possible versions of ourselves.

# BECOMING MORE EMOTIONALLY AVAILABLE

*The best and most beautiful things in the world cannot be seen or even touched. They must be felt with the heart.[1] ~ Anne Sullivan*

Becoming more emotionally available is just about the scariest thing I've ever done. Just telling one of my male friends at work that I'd missed him while he was on vacation brought me to a place in which I felt very unsettled and vulnerable. I seriously thought I might need to leave work for the day! Little by little, I felt more at ease. It was a very strange experience. I had to get used to the idea that when I express my feelings, things are still OK!

I met a man who helped me with the process of unfolding and feeling safe expressing my emotions—even emotions that made me feel as if I were two years old. I remember curling up in the fetal position with a blanket

---

[1]  From a letter, quoting her teacher (Anne Sullivan), dated June 8, 1891, from Helen Keller to the Reverend Phillips Brooks.

over my head. It was really bizarre! But you know what? Once I just felt these things, expressed them, and cried— howled even—I felt better. It was so scary and difficult. I felt so vulnerable. This was such a shift that it really took some getting used to. I went through stages of letting go of guilt for having and expressing my feelings. I felt so bad about troubling this man with my feelings. I felt emotionally safe with him and he made space for *all* my feelings, which helped me learn to make space for all my feelings and honor them. This also helped me learn to make space for other people's feelings too! I couldn't be- lieve it. It was amazing. He was amazing. And you know what? I was amazing. I was ready for this and I met some- one who was so willing and capable of helping me with it. I will never be able to express my immense gratitude for this experience, and for everyone who helped me to be able to have it, and to heal.

This opening up and becoming more emotionally available allowed me to learn to ask for what I want or need, to vulnerably express my fears (no matter how in- fantile they may seem), and to negotiate ways in which I can help other people meet their needs. I found I was able to give my children's feelings much more space and support. I was even beginning to be able to give Brian's feelings more space and support, as well.

Because I felt I could ask for help, I found that I was much more able to offer and give help. I didn't need to reserve most of my inner resources for myself because I could ask for help from others too. I was learning to give and receive freely! I was learning that the world around me was safe and that I could help and be helped. I learned that sharing and helping each other is a wonderful and connecting part of life. I no longer felt a scarcity about my inner resources. I felt abundance. I just could not believe that so much healing could take place within me, in less than a year's time. I was so happy. I could give myself permission to be all of myself, knowing that my feelings mattered and were important.

I came to a place where I could just say what I was feeling, in the moment, and it was wonderfully freeing. I no longer felt bad about anything I felt, said, or thought. These were just feelings, comments, and thoughts, after all, and they didn't define me. They were just experiences passing through me. Sometimes some of the things I said weren't the greatest, and sometimes they caused others pain because of how they were interpreted. But then I could be with the person and make space for their feelings and that was helpful. I would never intentionally hurt someone, and I knew that. I knew that within myself, and eventually, the other person knew that too.

I noticed that I acted like a mother to men in my life, and maybe a mother to everyone. I really don't know. I also don't know if that is how everyone else interpreted my actions, but that is how my actions felt to me. I think I'd always been a mother to my parents, growing up, and that is the only role I really remember having. I decided that I didn't want this role anymore. It was really a caretaking role in a lot of ways. It was disempowering to both parties, in my opinion. Not only did I stifle some of my feelings and needs to meet the expectations of others,

I was not 100 percent authentic, which probably supported inauthenticity in the other party too. It probably also enabled the other party not to see and find what they needed to find within themselves: essentially, I was supporting them to need me in some way. I obviously needed that experience, for whatever reason—but after this realization, I no longer did. I let others know my observations about myself and that I wanted to make a change. There was some expression of anxiety from a couple of people— those with whom I was closely involved. I said I needed to make the change and let them know that I thought everything would be OK. So I changed the ways in which I related to the men in my life, and to others, and I think I was supportive as I did so. It was wonderfully freeing, although scary at first. After the initial change, which was a bit painful for both parties, the people in my life really liked our evolved relationships! It was wonderful! It felt really, really good. What a huge relief!

Another thing I realized about myself is that I would let men lead. Whether it was a platonic friend or a lover, I would let him take the lead. I decided I would no longer do that. I trusted myself to lead myself. My inner authority about myself was growing stronger. So many positive things happened once I stopped letting men lead. One of the biggest changes is that I no longer need to worry about how Brian chooses to relate or is capable of relating to me. I can always treat him like he is a reasonable person who wants to work with me, no matter what! I'm truly free to have a loving divorce, regardless of what my ex-spouse chooses or is capable of. I have never been more truly free in my entire life. It is the best feeling!

I went through a tough time when I was letting go of some very dear beliefs I had. These beliefs were rather subconscious and it was painful to bring them out and negate them, and stop allowing them to run my life. It was really scary, too. I really believed that there was one person who could always be here for me. I thought I would find a magical someone who could always help me when I felt upset or help me when I was overwhelmed. Well, when I really admitted to myself my own limitations as a human being, I also admitted to myself the fact that all human beings have limitations. I think we can really try hard to be there for someone. Many of us put a lot of effort into that. But there is no way one person can always be there for another person. It seemed so sad to me, but it is so true. Illness, personal struggles, responsibilities, projects, and temporary distances can prevent a person from being able to help another. These are just a few possibilities.

Interestingly, I thought, if a person *could* accomplish always being there for someone else, what would the quality of their presence be? If that person never says no, that they are not in a good state of mind (or whatever) to be able to help, are they ever there for themselves? If they aren't, how are they supposed to be present, really present, for someone else? How could they be empathetic, really listen, and more? It seems that being able to be there for oneself may have something to do with whether or not a person can be emotionally and mentally present for someone else.

Speaking of subconscious beliefs, one day I was driving home and I was bringing some things to the surface about how it is OK if I don't have a boyfriend or husband. I was realizing that I had been carrying a lot of culturally and familially imposed judgments and ideas of my life being a mess if I didn't have a husband; I had no direction, or something really bad would happen and what would I do then? I realized that it is much more culturally acceptable for men to be single, at any age, than it is for women, at most ages, to be "unattached." I decided for myself that everything was OK if I had no boyfriend or husband. What a relief! I am always amazed at what is below the surface of my level of consciousness and how it really dictates my impulses and my life. Sheesh!

# LIFE!

I think life itself is creating all the time and that we create our lives each day. In order to create what fits me as an individual I've had to push through fears and try new things. I've had to grow and not be afraid to make mistakes—even public mistakes. Mistakes are our teachers but I think the fear of being wrong can keep many of us stagnant, unwilling to try new things. I've had to accept myself enough to make up for others' potential unacceptance of me and my choices. When we were young, we were probably taught that being different or doing things differently was wrong. In order to be oneself, I think a person must throw out this idea altogether. In order to be right, someone else doesn't have to be wrong. We can each do things our own way and still be OK—and thrive even. I think we live in a society that teaches that there is only one right way to do things and there is only one right answer. I think religion feeds this and our institutions carry it and feed it to the masses.

I hope that wherever you are and in whatever direction you are pointed, you know that there are so many others dealing with the same or similar struggles. We humans are an expression of life, free to express life in our own unique ways, if we only allow ourselves.

I feel so much less limited in my life because of my ability to be happily without a partner. My choices in my life can be *my* choices—they don't have to have someone else's "OK", and they don't have to "work" for someone else's life. My choices just have to be OK with me, and for now, also with my children. If I want something badly enough, fears will not limit my ability to achieve my dreams. After confronting many of my fears, I feel like my dreams can truly be whatever I want them to be! As I discover more fears, I can work through those too. In the future, if I want to volunteer to sift the sand in Egypt for months on end, I can do that. This might sound a bit extreme—but who knows, it might be something I want to do! I've actually thought about that before because I love archaeology. What are the chances there will be someone in my life who will want to do that same thing? I'd likely have to be able to be alone, travel alone, and function on my own if I wanted this, or possibly something equally unique, to be an option for me. And I want everything to be an option for me. This is my *life* I'm talking about, after all.

I'm a human being and precious few things are within my range of awareness, at any given moment and overall. It is tempting to try to avoid pain. I decided I wanted to go through my pain, rather than keep stuffing it down. It has been through this process that my awareness of some aspects of my emotional unavailability was born. It has been through this process that I have learned how to love people for who they are, not for who I thought they should be. What I used to think people should be was basically whatever would fit for me and enable me *not* to grow. That isn't good for anyone, but it fit with our often narcissistic, unhealthy culture.

I think this process has helped me to self-actualize more and more. I think it has helped me to hurt others less often. I also think it has helped me to be a better mother, in some ways.

I hope that you have your own unique vision of life and love, and that you have created or are in the process of creating that for yourself. I hope you consider that whether or not you find someone who holds the same vision you do, you can always create, have, and experience just the love you want, within yourself.

Here is my poem about love that I wrote several years ago. It was a dark and painful night—perhaps one of the most painful times in my life. I think some of the most beautiful things can come from times of darkness. My realization about love—my poem—has been an inspiration to me ever since, and it has helped me to make changes in my life that I feel good about, and that are more in line with what I feel love to be.

Love

All love wants is to observe,
Be present with that or whom
All love wants in return is to be observed,
Be present with that or whom
Real love is supporting
Real love doesn't need anything
It is happy with what is
That is love

For in love there is no lack
There is no aloneness
There is only contentment
There is only supporting
There is only thankfulness for what is

I AM love, available to BE
With or without someone
Enjoying, sharing life

Love is the space in which we observe
The space in which we play
The space in which we partake—
Without expectation

We are the space because
We are the observers
We are love, ready in waiting
Nothing exists without the observer;
Without the space in which to be, without--love

Every thing, every person is love
We think we have to find it
But it is all about seeing things or people
As they are
Not as we wish them to be

To know love
You just have to know what you are
If you find yourself,
You will find love
If you find love,
You will be content

Made in the USA
Middletown, DE
19 March 2016